GARDENS

AT FIRST LIGHT

GARDENS

AT FIRST LIGHT

STACY BASS

words by **JUDY OSTROW**

at**home**
BOOKS

A Division of Moffly Media | mofflymedia.com

PRODUCED BY

A Division of Moffly Media
205 Main Street
Westport, CT 06880
mofflymedia.com
athomebooks.com
Distributed by: National Book Network

Publisher: Jonathan Moffly
Executive Producer & Creative Director: Amy Vischio
Editor: Jeanne Craig
Art Director: Paula Winicur
Production Manager: Kerri Fice

10 9 8 7 6 5 4 3 2 1

Printed in Canada

ISBN 978-0-9862689-0-8

Library of Congress Number: 2015933591

"*There are some who bring a light so great to the world that even after they have gone, the light remains.*"
—AUTHOR UNKNOWN

**FOR MY DAD—
NEVER STOP SHINING**

CONTENTS

INTRODUCTION

There's something about the dawn. For me, it's the perfect time. It's quiet, reflective and kind. I can't pinpoint the exact moment I knew the dawn would be my muse, but then it just was. That first light gently caresses what lies before it and provides a fitting soundtrack for my photography. It's a subtle but energized hum that encourages me to be present, aware and focused, to connect to my surroundings in such a way that I can best share not only what was there before I stepped into the scene, but also how it felt to be in that space at that time.

As a young photographer, one of the ways I honed my craft was through attendance at the Maine Photographic Workshops, where seminars were taught by three masters: Jay Maisel, William Albert Allard and Joe Baraban. Though the spirit and direction of each person's work was very different, one of the key things I learned from all three of these artists is that light is the true master of any photographer. Chasing it to capture that once-in-a-lifetime moment, gesture or color is always worth the effort.

I know this to be true because I've spent countless mornings rising long before sunrise so I could be standing in a garden with camera in hand when the light appeared. Yes, scheduling these early morning photo shoots was often challenging (multiple rain dates were necessary), and often I worked on little sleep. Yet I'm convinced the dawn helped me portray each landscape in its very best light. As the book's title celebrates, all of the gardens featured in this volume were photographed at daybreak. Some of those mornings were crisp and clear, others were overcast or misty, but always the clarity and calm of that first light came through.

After the success of my first book, *In the Garden*, I spent the next two years thinking about whether I should begin work on a second title. I wondered if I had something more to share and if I did, was a book the best vehicle for my photographs. In the end, I couldn't resist the allure of a large and lavishly illustrated coffee-table book, one that invites the reader to linger on each page. Though I enjoy viewing pictures in the digital landscape—I, too, have a manageable fascination with Facebook and Instagram—there will always be a special and sacred place in my heart and mind for a beautiful, printed book.

Gardens at First Light is a sequel of sorts to *In the Garden* because the subject is nature photography. Yet as proud as I am of that first volume, with this second book I've tried to deliver even more. This book contains photographs of 12 incredible landscapes. Some are secret and intimate in size while others are grand and gorgeous, yet all of these gardens are unique as they reflect the enthusiasm and interests of the designers and homeowners who nurtured them. I hope that readers will be as mesmerized by these places as I was when I photographed them.

Along with hundreds of images of lush landscapes, this book offers delightful background on each property. Writer Judy Ostrow talked with the people who brought each garden to life and the information she culled will surely resonate with those who have a passion for nature. In addition, a reference guide at the back of the book presents a more detailed picture of how each garden is arranged. This is the type of section that's meant to inspire avid gardeners who are curating ideas for their own landscapes.

It's my hope that you'll be encouraged to spend more time investigating and experiencing the special gardens featured here, and that you'll return to the book, time and again, for the visual pleasure that comes at first light.

–STACY BASS, JANUARY 2015

"Awake the dawn that sleeps in heaven; let light
Rise from the chambers of the east, and bring
The honey'd dew that cometh on waking day.
O radiant morning; salute the sun."

—WILLIAM BLAKE, "TO MORNING"

GREEN LEGACY

Every previous owner of the classic brick home of Jane Alison Dunn and her husband, Vaughn Dunn, has added something to it that reflects their own interests. For one owner, who transformed the original 1928 clapboard structure with brick cladding, her love of tennis fueled the completion of a competition-worthy court. Another steward of the property installed a solarium as an antidote to Northeastern winters. When the Dunns bought the house and its five-plus acres seven years ago, Jane knew it would be an excellent canvas for the passion she's nurtured since childhood: gardening.

The home's facade presents an elegant Georgian face to the world. Enhancing that welcome is a tiered fountain that's centered in the entry court and surrounded by a circular walk created with granite pavers and a boxwood parterre. Roses mark the way to the front door of the house. With a penchant for human-scaled garden rooms, Jane skillfully drew the perimeters for the terraces, patio, kitchen garden and other distinctive enclaves that surround the house. The boundaries for these spaces were created with trees, evergreen hedges and other border plants, all of which contribute to the serenity of each garden room. From a distance, each room seems to connect with its neighbor seamlessly. It's only when viewed in close-up—as you happen upon a set of stairs or a change of pavers—that these hidden links become evident. Like a symphony, this landscape has great harmony.

There's consonance in her design, and it's achieved with a cheerful palette: there are delicate pastels from flowering bulbs in early spring; pink, white and blue blooms in summer, and a grand show of hues in high season. Depending upon the time of year, great expanses of some of her perennial favorites greet the eye: tulips in spring, roses and peonies a bit later, and hydrangeas everywhere in midsummer. Thanks to a glassed-in "plant hospital" and two heated bays of the garage—areas reserved for plants that need extra care or warmth in the winter—some prized annuals return to the garden with each growing season. One of these is the clear azure plumbago (*Plumbago auriculata* 'Royal Cape'), which normally frequents the warmer zones of the country but is irresistible in its profuse bloom habit. Jane places some at various entry points of the garden rooms.

Flowers occupy a sizable section of Jane's domain, but they are by no means the entire story of this property. Just as her mother grew vegetables and planted an apple tree for each of her five children, Jane has dedicated a generous portion of the landscape to a kitchen herb garden, a fenced-in produce garden and a nascent orchard, with a tended beehive to assist in pollination. The Dunns' fruit tree assortment includes such heirloom apple varieties as Albemarle Pippin and Esopus Spitzenburg, two trees that Thomas Jefferson grew himself at Monticello and from which he made cider. There are also two peach and two cherry trees. Among the vegetables are numerous healthy choices including eggplant, peppers, beans, Swiss chard, kale and tomatoes. Anything not used in her kitchen will go to friends. Some of Jane's most appreciated gifts are jars of tomato sauce and small containers of honey from her bee colony.

A walk around this landscape is a pleasure in its own right, yet much of the enjoyment of the Dunn garden is Jane's own sincere appreciation of her surroundings and her happy willingness to freely give her knowledge and her bounty to others. It's a talent that she shares with so many of the most devoted gardeners, enthusiasts who are often as generous in spirit as they are creative with the land.

Buxus 'Green Mountain' stand at the back terrace that's abloom with a dozen varieties of peonies; some dark pink blooms are 'Mabel Gore' and 'Elsie Pickett.' Among the light pink varieties are 'Eden's Perfume,' 'Sarah Bernhardt,' 'Bowl of Beauty,' and 'Monsieur Jules Elie.' The white is 'Festiva Maxima,' which has tiny specks of red.

The approach to the house is marked by a parterre centered with a four-tiered fountain and ringed by a low hedge of *Buxus* 'Green Gem.' The wrought iron fence near the house is lined with 'Knock Out' roses in shades of rose and pink. The front walk is flanked by two circular French stone containers (one is visible here) filled with blue agapanthus and a variety of white annuals.

Flanking the doors of the greenhouse is a pair of *Hydrangea macrophylla* 'Endless Summer.'
To the right stand two honeybee hives that yield a harvest of 75 pounds
of honey per year. Beyond the hives, there is a glimpse of the orchard.

The trees in planters on the pink limestone-paved pool terrace are *Hydrangea paniculata* 'Tardiva' standards, underplanted with a combination of light and dark pink annuals, such as petunias, verbena, lobularia and dipladenia. Purple spikes of *Nepeta racemosa* 'Walker's Low' are planted in front of the wall, near an assortment of lilies not yet in bloom.

On the eastern terrace, various types of arborvitae frame the space like a gathering of old friends. To the right, giant boxwoods, moved from the owners' previous home, complete the perimeter.

ABOVE: *Digitalis purpurea*—also known as foxglove—in full bloom. **OPPOSITE:** The kitchen garden faces due east, with southern magnolia espaliered trees against the brick wall. The tall purple flowers in the back of this garden are a combination of delphinium varieties. In the foreground are rows of allysum, *Heuchera* 'Snow Angel,' and a mixture of snapdragons in shades of pink and white. In the far right corner is a prized *Echeveria elegans*, or Mexican Snowball.

OPPOSITE: Instead of hoops, the homeowners prefer to use stakes and string to hold up the heavy heads of the peony flowers in long beds. **THIS PAGE:** *Paeonia lactiflora* 'Charles Burgess,' an old and much-prized variety of peony, was inherited from the previous owners of the property. It flourishes in a very sheltered area with a western exposure.

The angel urn is one of a pair that flanks a brick walkway to the glass tennis pavilion. The owners call this lush outdoor room their west tennis court garden, a spot where they serve afternoon tea. The urn is filled with *Mandevilla x amabilis* 'Alice Du Pont,' white *Calibrachoa* 'Million Bells,' and *Scaevola aemula* 'Whirlwind.'

LEFT: Three varieties of clematis intertwine along this brick wall: 'Jackmanii,' 'King Fisher,' and 'Ice Blue.' RIGHT: The gazebo was custom-designed and erected in the early 1980s. The tree behind it is a *Gleditsia triacanthos* 'Sunburst,' or honey locust. It's constantly pruned to keep its shape. The urns are filled with mandevilla, dipladenia and *Lobularia* 'Snow Princess.'

LEFT: Espaliered *Pyracantha angustifolia*, in flower, has been trained in a lattice pattern to fit perfectly inside a brick border on one wall of the courtyard in front of the house. **TOP**: A close-up of *Allium* 'Globemaster,' which can be found in both the kitchen garden and west tennis court garden. **ABOVE**: *Lamium maculatum* 'Purple Dragon,' which Jane loves for its beautiful foliage; she'll dig some up to put in containers with annuals, then replant in garden soil in the fall.

ON THE ROCKS

Rock ledges and outcroppings distinguish the peninsulas and islands along the New England coast, including one spectacular parcel. The current owners of this prime piece of waterfront property were drawn to its remarkable features, including a splendid view of Long Island Sound, an ambling path to a summit overlooking that vista, and a perennial garden growing among the boulders.

Soon after they bought the property, the owners met and hired the woman who had maintained the landscape for two previous owners. From the age of 18, Heather O'Neill developed her gardening and design skills on this acreage, coaxing its natural beauty to emerge. Along the way, she acquired professional credentials, studying horticulture at the New York Botanical Gardens. For some 20 years, Heather has combined her talents with her clients' own affection for the varied, rocky topography of this site. Using the raw materials of ledges and trees sculpted by wind and water, she crafted spaces for relaxation and entertaining. When a contiguous parcel of land came on the market—and with it, the possibility for the current owners to build a new home at the apex of the land's rise above the shore—Heather was on board for the challenge. This piece of coast, now expanded to five acres, had the potential to become an extraordinary seaside estate.

Today, a stately stone manor house of recent vintage (but looking as if it has always dominated its hilltop site) is at the end of the winding drive from the front gates. While the house has a commanding presence, there are many elements in its landscape that are worth pausing to see in the journey to the entry court. Colorful floral displays and shapely specimen trees provide many beautiful views. The owners—who love the mature trees that enrich the landscape, particularly in the summer when cooling sea breezes rustle their leaves—were reluctant to displace these features for construction of the new stone house. Instead, they took extra caution to protect them. They also sought to preserve as much of the rock as was possible.

When the house was complete, Heather accentuated its perimeters with the boxwood and floral borders that its formal profile demanded. But farther from the house, a less-structured approach to garden design took over. Around many ledges, Heather simply sculpted an edge of lawn, preferring to accent the rocks' unadorned, rugged planes. In other spots, she filled the cracks and crevices of outcroppings with sturdy plants that could thrive despite the wind, salt and shallow soil—creeping phlox, sedum, dianthus and many others. Over time, these naturalized beds have produced great sweeps of color and texture.

As the landscape has developed, the owners have indulged their passion for beautiful trees, adding new silhouettes of unusual specimens at key places, using them as backdrops or co-mingling conifers with flowering plants and shrubs to dramatic effect. Such eye-catching trees as Kousa dogwood, magnificent copper beech and *Acer japonicum* 'Taki no gawa' (also known as full moon maple, with its exquisite chartreuse foliage) have become fixtures here.

With all of the major elements in place, the homeowners make a point of walking the grounds with Heather each spring and fall. During these treks, the trio plan for the coming season and decide what might need to be tweaked, moved or replaced. For Heather, who credits the property with her own growth as a designer, and the owners, for whom its evolving features have become a passion, this promontory is a work in progress and the bedrock for future delights.

Rock formations indigenous to the Northeastern coast create foundations for many of the flower beds. Burgundy, lollipop-like blooms are *Allium sphaerocephalum*. Also in the mix are purple platycodon, blue salvia, yellow *Zinnia* 'Profusion,' and *Pentas lanceolata*, a white, low-growing annual.

Great cascades of colorful perennials bloom throughout the growing season, including the display of *Hydrangea macrophylla* 'Endless Summer,' and *Astilbe* 'Vision Pink' at lower left. The landscape is further punctuated with pretty specimen trees, such as the young Kousa dogwood (*Cornus kousa*) in the center.

With its heavenly blue color, *Hydrangea serrata* 'Bluebird' mingles with other perennials, as well as the small cedars that sprout up unexpectedly around the property. The owners usually leave the cedars and let nature do its own landscaping.

The tiny interior flowers of *Hydrangea serrata* 'Bluebird' are fertile, while
the larger exterior blooms are sterile. If they are left on their stems into the fall,
the drying sterile blooms will turn a lovely shade of lavender.

The landscape designer cleared a long rock formation that was full of weeds and added soil in the crevices, making room for flowers. In shallow soil to the left of the red 'Knock Out' rosebush are clumps of spiky *Angelonia* in pink and white. These tropicals are often used as annuals in the gardens of the Northeast.

OPPOSITE: Mixed in with *Astilbe* and varieties of *Athyrium*, nature's own moss is part of the setting. **THIS PAGE:** The restored barn, renovated by the current owners, has become an entertaining space.

This particularly tall variety of Shasta daisy—*Leucanthemum x superbum* 'Becky'—takes root easily in the shallow soil of certain sections of the rock garden beds. Drifts of these sturdy perennials were planted. From afar, their petals create a confetti effect among the other plants in the garden.

A perimeter garden with pops of white from Shasta daisies meanders toward the rocky shore. The floral show begins in spring with an explosion of bulbs that are replaced in summer with a profusion of perennials.

THE EDIBLE GARDEN

When the oldest of her children was about to begin kindergarten, Phoebe Cole-Smith moved her family from New York City to a small town in Connecticut. Not quite ready for a typical house on a suburban cul de sac, she found a wooded property along an unpaved road. The vintage dwelling that went with it had possibilities, as did the land. Phoebe visualized a garden that would enhance the setting and enable her to produce home-grown food for her family.

Both her family and the garden grew up around the house, its large, welcoming kitchen an indication of the importance given to the preparation of good, fresh food. To an old perennial garden already on the property, Phoebe added annuals, plus beds for herbs and vegetables. She also built a chicken coop; the hens gave her eggs and plenty of organic fertilizer. She made friends among the farmers at the local outdoor market, who gave her advice about growing things. When her children entered high school, Phoebe enrolled in cooking school. In a stroke of synchronization, part of her training was an internship at the now-renowned Blue Hill at Stone Barns restaurant in Tarrytown, New York, a pioneer in the farm-to-table movement. When she finished her training, Phoebe began using her garden produce to cater meals and parties. Eventually, a business was born. Today, her menus are unique as they feature her organically grown vegetables, such as red-and-white 'French Breakfast' radishes and purple-veined 'Red Giant' mustard leaves.

Everything about the Cole-Smith garden is just a bit off the beaten path, and delightfully so. To get there, you travel from a four-lane highway to an asphalt country road and finally to the unpaved lane that leads to Dirt Road Farm—the name Phoebe gave to both her land and then her growing business.

The summer gardens are filled with flowers that thrive in the southern New England climate: coneflower (*Echinacea purpurea*), black-eyed Susan (*Rudbeckia hirta*), a veritable blanket of nasturtiums (*Tropaeolum*), and dozens more. The faint hum of bees—Phoebe keeps hives for pollination and honey—and the gentle clucking of chickens mingle with birdsong and leaves rustling in the breeze. A deep patio outside the kitchen is sized for gathering robust harvests and serving big feasts. An enormous vine that twists its way around a sheltering pergola makes concord grapes as well as shade. The flower gardens, a crazy quilt of annuals and perennials, decorate the spaces around the food plots and provide the raw materials for bouquets that grace the tables at events catered by Phoebe. At Dirt Road Farm, everything is productive, in a most joyful concert of taste, aroma and color.

Even the stand of sugar maples that covers three of the property's five-and-a-half acres has its job to do. Five winters ago, Phoebe gifted her husband, Mike, with a kit that included three buckets and three taps. Today, they have 150 taps and an evaporator that can process 300 gallons of sap in eight hours. She says maple syrup production is labor-intensive, requiring a warmly dressed crew of about 40 family and friends, but the reward is sublime syrup to accompany her pancakes.

Phoebe's expansion plans continue. There's a small plot of fruit trees on her land; they're still too young for fruit-bearing, but like the heirloom seeds she collects, sows and grows for her menus, the fruit will soon be full of flavor. An old shed will be transformed to a petite commercial kitchen, where she'll produce more of the food she's become known for. Her garden is a fine case of inspiration meeting opportunity, and Phoebe is quick to say it's great to do what one loves.

Of the two dozen chickens that occupy the Cole-Smith coop and enclosure, Gertrude, a pure white French Marans hen, is one of the original group of fifteen chicks that the homeowners picked up at Burr Farm in Hampton, Connecticut, in 2011. They're not sure if she's the alpha hen—the one at the top of the pecking order—but her pristine appearance signifies she's in the first tier of the free-ranging flock.

LEFT: The enormous white-flowering shrub at the back of this large bed that's used for cutting is *Hydrangea paniculata*, one of a pair gifted to the homeowner many years ago for Mother's Day; she's unsure of the variety, though guesses it's 'Unique.' **BELOW:** In addition to the flourishing *Echinacea augustifolia*, *Rudbeckia hirta* (black-eyed Susan) happily spreads out.

The perennial gardens offer masses of flowers for wildlife and Phoebe's vases. Growing up around the armillary are stalks of plume poppies (*Macleaya cordata*), a rhizome-spreading plant that bees love.

ABOVE: From left to right are three of Phoebe's favorites, *Zinnia elegans* 'Benary's Giant,' *Helianthus annus*
'Van Gogh,' which is an heirloom sunflower with a shiny green center, and another heirloom, *Lilium martagon* 'Black Beauty.'
OPPOSITE: Zinnias are enchanting in every stage of bloom, as this multilayered bud reveals.

THIS PAGE: Some of the day's harvest includes 'Tavera' French green beans, 'Calypso' pickling cukes, 'Guardsman Chioggia' beets, tricolor carrots 'Circus, Circus,' and Blue African basil, all organically grown. **OPPOSITE:** A Concord grape vine hugs the pergola, nasturtiums twine in the foreground and Meyer lemon plants sprout from patio containers.

THIS PAGE: Two forms of natural pest control
are chickens and the marigolds planted in the
vegetable garden to deter unwanted insects.
The large orange-flowered variety seen inside
the enclosure is *Tagetes erecta* 'Giant Orange.'
OPPOSITE: Breakfast is a locavore's delight
as all ingredients hail from this garden and
others nearby. The lemonade in the Mason jar
dispenser is flavored with Blue African basil.

THIS PAGE: An early heirloom dahlia, 'Old Gold.' **OPPOSITE:** The homeowners made these supports for winter squash, and have since improved their design for added strength.

Local craftsman William Rowe built the Adirondack-style enclosure several years ago; he learned this construction method building furniture and fences in that part of upstate New York. The wire mesh portion doesn't extend deep in the soil but does deter large critters.

GARDEN RENEWAL

In search of a house close to her office, Ann Klee and her husband, John Macleod, happened upon a nearly new home that was well constructed and in a fine location. They snapped it up. Since it was already fully landscaped, there was little need to do anything else. Ann and John fenced a portion of the yard to provide a safe space for their dogs, and they installed a screened-in patio from which they could admire their new property and its delightful sunken garden surrounded by stone walls.

While everything about the house and its amenities seemed perfectly 21st century, the couple soon learned it had an interesting backstory. In the 1920s and '30s, the area was home to many large estates, and the Macleod/Klee property was a piece of a relatively big one. The original house—which was made part of another parcel when the estate was subdivided—was the creation of Cameron Clark, an architect known for the stately and classic homes that are still prized in the Northeast. His wife, Agnes Selkirk Clark, had developed her own following for her landscape work. As it turned out, she had created a sunken garden for this particular lot. To the surprise of the former owners of John and Ann's house, construction of a pool revealed the old boundaries and beds of this vintage landscape element. Having admired its stone perimeters, the older trees planted in and around it, and an ancient wisteria vine, their instinct was to restore it.

In this venture the former owners found a willing partner in Kim Proctor, whom they happened to meet through her son, Ross. While buying trees and shrubs at the local nursery where Ross worked, these owners told him about the old garden. He suggested the couple call his mother, Kim, who had studied at the Rhode Island School of Design and worked at her stepfather's nursery during breaks from art school. Her interest in art and plants began to merge, and then evolved into a career as a landscape designer.

Proctor began work on the property by installing new elements, including a hardscape, foundation plantings and specimen trees. When those projects drew to a close, she was ready to focus on the vintage garden. The former homeowners had not been able to locate Agnes Clark's design for their landscape, but a source at the local historical society helped them discover a key connection.

Agnes Clark had worked for another well-known landscape architect, Ellen Biddle Shipman. Because Shipman's work had been well preserved, Kim could piece together some of the ideas that inspired the sunken garden, and plants that may have originally grown there. Understanding that manageable maintenance made sense for her clients, Kim installed substitutes for the many labor-intensive flowering plants that would have filled the original garden. Evergreens and shrubs became an important part of its structure, including boxwood, hydrangea, spirea and Japanese plum yew. Using a carefully edited color palette, Kim added perennials to the mix. While the space is not huge, it occupies a spot on the property with a spectrum of microclimates, from wet and shady to dry and sun-drenched. Thus, Kim made plantings accordingly.

When John and Ann bought the property from the former owners, they knew little about horticulture, but they appreciated the beauty of the work completed by Kim. The two new stewards respect what came before them. With professions that keep them very busy, one of their pleasures is to sit around the fire pit they've added at the end of the pool in the historic garden. When talking about how he and Ann view their landscape, and Agnes Clark's peaceful garden, John will often say it restores their souls and their sanity.

Atop the pergola in the vintage garden is a wisteria vine that most likely dates to the 1930s. Unobstructed by trees, it blooms abundantly in spring.

LEFT: The shade of an old but still vigorous *Cornus florida* creates one of the microclimates in this garden. Varieties of astilbe and *Hosta* 'August Moon' thrive in their locations; *Paeonia lactiflora* 'Krinkled White' prefers the sunnier spots. **BELOW:** Containers sprout with sweet potato vines.

THIS PAGE: Blue-violet is a prominent hue among the plants in the restored garden. *Clematis* 'The President' climbs a perimeter wall with the help of a trellis; this variety has large flowers and a long blooming season. Beside it grows a thriving clump of spiky *Salvia nemerosa* 'Caradonna.' **OPPOSITE:** This clematis, striking in summer, offers interest in fall, with attractive seed heads.

LEFT: The early light lends a rosy appearance to the blue-violet salvia; the low round plants in front of them are *Buxus sinica var. insularis* 'Tide Hill,' a low-growing dwarf Korean boxwood that functions almost like a ground cover.
BELOW: At right, clumps of *Liriope muscari* 'Variegata' grow beneath the trio of tall arborvitae that are original to the garden. In the background are some highlights of a neighbor's property, including the pale lavender blooms of what the landscape designer believes is a Preston lilac hybrid.

The landscape designer chose the combination of pink *Spiraea bumalda* 'Gold Mound' and *Salvia nemerosa* 'Caradonna' for their color, ease of cultivation, long bloom time and love of full sun. The foliage of the spiraea has a golden color that contrasts nicely with the many deep-green plants.

LEFT: At the eastern edge of the landscape, a footbridge crosses a small stream; even though this path continues onto an adjoining property, it provides a visual extension. The low plants in the foreground are *Monarda* 'Petite Delight,' a dwarf bee balm that blooms later in the season. The large plant at right is *Aesculus parviflora*, or bottlebrush buckeye. To the left of the path is a patch of shade-loving eastern wood fern, or *Dyopteris marginalis*. **ABOVE:** The annual *Calibrachoa* 'Blue,' also known as million bells, replaces salvia for late-summer color.

Containers of annuals—a double impatiens variety called 'Silhouette Red'— line a path along the back of the walled enclosure. The dogwood at right is flanked by two *Ilex verticillata* 'Sparkleberry,' a shrub with red berries that provides interest in winter and food for hungry birds.

PICTURE PERFECT

When Stacy Bass talks about her work as a nature photographer, questions invariably arise about her own garden. Until a few years ago, her honest answer was "I don't have one." But after completing a makeover of the house she shares with her husband, Howard, and their four children, she was ready to tackle the landscape.

Facing a tidal inlet, the back of the house required a garden that would synchronize with the natural beauty beyond the property lines. At the front of the house, there was minimal space for plantings. To find the right person for the project, Stacy searched through the long list of professionals she'd met over the years. A great partnership emerged when she connected with Sean Jancski, a landscape architect in Rye, New York. He understood her vision for a contemporary garden strong on texture, shape and layering. He also knew Stacy's home had been remade for a seamless transition from indoors to out. Thus, the landscape would function as an extension of the interior's clean aesthetic.

Spare and simple forms—as well as water- and weather-tolerant natural materials—create the palette for the hardscape at the back of the house. Jancski designed a pool with a double infinity edge along the far side of its perimeter. As a result, the pool appears to flow toward the inlet beyond when viewed from the dining area. Underfoot, ipe decking feels soft in the summer months, but wears well in the harsher seasons. The low-key and linear plan provides all the comforts of outdoor living, and enhances the beautiful surroundings rather than competing with them. The overall impression feels both modern and zen.

Paths at either end of the house offer lessons in shade planting. Fences are engulfed by lush green walls of euonymus. While wisteria bursts with blossoms in late spring (climbing over a discreetly placed outdoor shower), most of the plants lining the walkway toward the front of the property provide interest with their varied leaf shapes and shades of green. A row of Japanese forest grass with yellow-green leaves illuminates the path with color alone. That's one example of Stacy's love of elegant, surprising detail. It can be found in personal touches throughout the landscape. Walkway lighting, for instance, is of delicate design. There are beautifully crafted gateposts, too, which are urban contemporary and mirror the home's modern take on Shingle style.

The same simple aesthetic at the back of the house is showcased on the street side. Along the front of the property are three pocket gardens; in each, layers of variegated greenery and geometric plantings create the background for sculptural works that surprise and delight passersby. The focal point is a spherical fountain, a shimmering orb that draws the eye to its illuminated movement. It's flanked by a gleaming metallic disc in one corner of the lot and a modern bench for quiet contemplation in the other. The front gardens have a sophisticated symmetry that's well-suited for an artist like Stacy, who appreciates order and beautiful form.

As with all great gardens, joy comes in using them. Stacy's family really lives in this landscape. But, even though the back side of the house is spectacular for its just-right functionality and amazing coastal setting, the photographer and her family take pleasure in the three front gardens, with their jewel-like centerpieces. Stacy's favorite time to be out there is after the lawn has just been cut and she can hear the quiet trickle of water in the fountain. She loves the calm and says the garden supplies the perfect backdrop for a reflective life.

Structural pieces anchor three pocket gardens in front of the house. The owner chose this magical orb fountain by artist Allison Armour as the focal point of the central space. She discovered Armour's work while photographing another garden.

The front yard faces the owners' guest house across the street. Low rounds of *Buxus sempervirens* are used for borders and blend with other sculptural shapes, including arborvitae. The smoothly pruned hornbeams provide variety in form. A variegated grass—*Liriope muscari* 'Variegata'—creates a counterpoint in texture.

OPPOSITE: In one pocket garden, David Harber's stainless-steel sculpture, Torus, is framed by the wintercreeper, *Euonymous fortunei* 'Emerald Gaiety,' and *Spiraea japonica* 'Little Princess.' **ABOVE:** Layered ground cover includes *Ajuga reptans* 'Burgundy Glow' in the foreground. **BELOW:** Some shapely forms in this garden are *Heuchera* 'Lime Marmalade,' *Echinacea purpurea* 'Alba,' and *Euonymous fortunei* 'Manhattan.'

Simple, contemporary fixtures were installed to light paths on the property. To soften the joints between bluestone pavers, *Thymus serphyllum*, or creeping thyme, was planted between the stones. The plant can be used this way in areas with moderate foot traffic.

OPPOSITE: A third pocket garden at the front of the house centers around a bench designed by Massimo Vignelli. This sheltered seat is flanked by two enormous masses of *Miscanthus sinensis* 'Gracillimus,' or maiden grass. **THIS PAGE:** The outdoor shower's stone wall is made of thin-stacked ashlar-pattern native fieldstone; *Hakenochloa macra* 'Aureola' grows along the path to the front of the house. The dark-leafed tree above the walk and over the shower is a *Prunus cerasifera*, or purple leaf plum.

THE GRADUAL GARDEN

Every garden plan starts somewhere. For Michael and Beazie Larned, a simple gift of Jacob's ladder from their daughter's nursery school teacher back in 1978 became the genesis of a garden that now covers a large portion of the couple's five-plus-acre homestead. The plant found a home in the couple's Valley Garden—the first plot they developed, located close to the house. Beazie added goat's beard and late-blooming autumn snakeroot to the plot in that first season. Thirty-six years later, the Larneds have produced a mature landscape that reflects their individual leanings and honors the terrain of their home in Connecticut. The varied topography and masses of rock ledge that surround their circa 1797 house offer panoramic views, and there are a number of microclimates and soils that have enabled them to cultivate a broad spectrum of plants, shrubs and trees. Yet one of the most interesting and significant collections in this garden began with a single evergreen that was planted before the Larneds' arrival.

Michael found a slow-growing Japanese umbrella pine—its common name—that struck him as attractive and interesting. But after a weeklong course in 1998 that was taught by conifer experts, everything changed for him. The more he learned about that evergreen tree (*Sciadopitys verticillata*), the more fascinated he became with conifers in general. Smitten by this branch of the plant kingdom, Michael acquired several hundred rare and beautiful specimens in subsequent years. Today, distinctive conifers display their varied foliage throughout the property. Michael also arranged some notable trees in dedicated plots that enhance their forms and textures.

As Michael's passion for conifers evolved, Beazie applied her skills as a quilter to add flowering plants and shrubs to the multiplying beds around their property. She believes gardens and quilts are about design, color, scale, pattern and texture. To keep her garden harmonious, she repeated colors, but used different plants. Likewise, in quilting, she's used many different prints, but always controlled the color.

An enormous rock formation at a high elevation became the site of one of the couple's most ambitious projects. The Larneds' daughters had dubbed it Mole Mountain when they played there as children, and it possessed possibilities and challenges. The Larneds wanted to accentuate its dramatic presence with interesting plantings. A gentle winter in 2001 gave them the opportunity to strip away vegetation, topsoil and boulders, although they reserved those natural materials for reuse at a later date. Today, a winding path climbs Mole Mountain. Walk that path to the summit and you're surrounded by alpine plantings and conifers, and offered an easy survey of daylily and wildflower beds. There also are views to the woods and the vegetable gardens. From the bridge that connects Mole Mountain to their barn—also Michael's office—you can look down onto shade plantings, each with ample protection from the sun so they can thrive.

In this garden, the Larneds have masterfully employed exposures and elevations to their best possible use. Even a west-facing expanse of rock ledge—a harsh environment for many plants—has been put to work warming the meditation garden in the less-cultivated, southeastern part of the property.

They've been making their garden for more than three decades, yet Michael and Beazie continue to discover fresh ideas. It's not unusual to find the couple moving things around and keeping others in a holding pattern, resting in pots under a pergola near the herb garden. For plant specimens in this lush landscape, life is a meandering journey. As Michael likes to say, one thing always leads to another.

The owners replaced a hot flagstone patio with a sheltering structure they call Arbor House. The vine climbing its latticed sides is *Hydrangea anomala petiolaris*. To the left of the house, a *Sciadopitys verticillata*, or Japanese umbrella pine, shows off its unique foliage year-round. In the foreground are pink blooms of *Lychnis coronaria*.

OPPOSITE: Below the pool is a terraced garden where *Sedum spectabile* grows between stones in the retaining wall; above is a mix of perennials, including *Stokesia laevis* 'Colorwheel' and *Knautia macedonica*. **THIS PAGE:** *Tradescantia ohiensis*; the annual *Cleome spinosa*; and *Platycodon grandiflorus* 'Sentimental Blue,' which blooms beside the supersized Star of Persia, *Allium christophii*.

Along the western edge of the rock formation dubbed Mole Mountain are the showy blossoms of the shrub *Aesculus parviflora*. In the background, three *Metasequoia glyptostroboides*, or dawn redwood trees, glow beacon-like with their golden needles.

THIS PAGE: A highbush blueberry (*Vaccinum corymbosum* 'Earliblue') produces fruit in early July, extending the growing season when it's planted in combination with species that ripen later.
OPPOSITE: On the east side of Mole Mountain, *Verbascum thapsus* blooms in the foreground. The alpine conifer garden includes the yellow-tipped *Chamaecyparis obtusa* 'Crippsii,' the small, rounded *Pinus densiflora* 'Jane Kluis,' and two tall, vertical *Thuja occidentalis*.

THIS PAGE: The alpine garden also contains a collection of miniature and dwarf conifers. Growing out of the wall at the edge of the gravel path are *Cymbalaria muralis*, *Campanula portenschlagiana* and *Aquilegia canadensis*.
OPPOSITE: *Hemerocallis* 'Winsome Lady' is just one of a varied collection of daylilies in the Larned garden.

Prominent features in this part of the garden are framed by a pin oak (*Quercus palustris*) on the left and a Japanese stewartia tree (*Stewartia pseudocamellia*) on the right. Just behind the pin oak is the fenced entrance to the vegetable and herb gardens, with a hedge of *Fagus sylvatica purpurea* (copper beech) and *Clematis montana* 'Rubens' on the arbor.

THIS PAGE: *Monarda didyma* 'Jacob Cline' is a tall and vigorous bee balm that provides nectar and seed for birds from its red flowers; its dense foliage offers cover for wildlife.
OPPOSITE: This view from Mole Mountain shows the diversity of plant material on the property. The full planting beds and mature trees attest to the owners' dedicated commitment to the landscape.

THIS PAGE: This variety of purple coneflower, *Echinacea purpurea* 'Magnus', has large petals and is an excellent cutting flower. **OPPOSITE:** At top left, beside the beech hedge, is the conifer *Pinus densiflora* 'Oculus Draconis,' or dragon's eye pine. This variety of the Japanese red pine has unique needles with alternating bands of yellow and green. They create some warmth in a winter landscape.

A bench sits beneath the native *Cornus florida rubra*. To the left and below the path's border of *Vinca minor* and other ground cover is the low-growing *Juniperus virginiana* 'Grey Owl' with its horizontal growing habit. Birds enjoy the berries from its female plants. Hanging from the dogwood above the bench is a birdhouse made from a home-grown gourd.

SERENE SYMMETRY

About fifteen years ago, Elizabeth and John Fath bought a 1939 house built in the French manor style. They were excited about its classic lines and fine details. It also had a great provenance, with the design rendered by Cameron Clark, a popular local architect of that era. The surrounding property, however, was less inspiring. When the Faths called in landscape designer Rob Wilber, his professional eye saw beyond the hodgepodge of minimal plantings and visualized the potential of the long, rectangular lot.

The main portion of Rob's design addressed the shape of the property—its length far exceeded its width. He had to provide a way to connect back to front without what might seem to be an endless walk to the pool area at the far end. His solution was a series of three formal garden rooms that would succeed one another in an artful procession, a design he'd execute with a two-foot rise in the grade of the lawn.

Today, the first garden room is located just beyond the back terrace at the rear of the house. The center room that follows is nearly out of sight, until you walk halfway across the lawn to a series of steps that lead to it. Then, passing through a viburnum hedge, there are more steps that take you down to the pool area. This sequence of rooms provides a formal and orderly arrangement, one that lends itself to a restrained palette of hardscape materials, plants and colors. Traditional favorites are on view here: climbing roses and clematis, sedum and salvia, viburnum and verbena. Garden rooms and paths are punctuated with delightful ornaments, many of which Elizabeth discovered in antiques shops.

In the center garden room, two umbrella-shaped forms—they were modeled by Rob's nursery to support plants that wind and climb—are filled with a pretty New England rose,

a pink Meidiland variety. Pink is definitely a theme in this garden; perennials and annuals are disciplined to a range that runs from the palest blush to deepest magenta. Even the linens and cushions in the pool house beautifully echo the scheme of pink and green. The colorway starts at the door leading from the house to the back terrace, which is flanked by two exquisite, rosy-colored mandevilla. It concludes under the pool arbor with a pair of giant-leafed *Colocasia esculenta* 'Illustris,' the dramatic elephant's ear.

Behind the pool arbor, a gate leads to an enclosed vegetable garden and less formal spaces. Turn left at that garden and you'll find the shade of old trees and a meandering moss-covered path. Turn right to wind your way back to the pool house and the formal enclosures. Some areas in the Fath landscape have been thoughtfully reserved for a closer commune with nature, including an intimate conversation spot under a beautiful Korean dogwood, where a pair of old, weathered chairs beckon.

A few years ago, Elizabeth asked another local designer, Alice Cooke, to bring more interest to the street side of the property. Alice obliged with structured plantings that honor the vintage French architectural flavor of the house and add dramatic footnotes to the already graceful landscape. While a large and beautiful copper beech still provides its majestic shade at the front entry, Alice enhanced the classic facade with a row of hornbeams, boxwood hedge, evergreen *Magnolia grandiflora* for a privacy screen and even more traditional greenery. It is a compliment to the Faths and to their partners in landscape design that the home's original owners—two collectors of French antiques who wanted a pretty and proper place for their special treasures—would feel completely at ease in this remarkable landscape.

Hedges and stone walls lend an appealing sense of order to the main areas of the landscape. Here, *Buxus sempivirens* is trimmed with graceful curves to accommodate finials found at an antiques shop.

The landscape designer created a series of three garden rooms for this long, rectangular property. The photographer is standing in the first room; the second is filled with pink flowers; the third is anchored by the pool and enhanced by a rose-covered arbor and a gate. The camera foreshortens the length of each room; it's a long walk from the house to the pool.

OPPOSITE: A tranquil space in the shade of a beautifully shaped *Cornus kousa* makes an ideal spot for a conversation, with a fire saucer for warmth on cool evenings. The vintage pair of Adirondack chairs have a patina created by age and the benign covering of lichen fungi. **THIS PAGE:** An echeveria-filled cast concrete container (left) is surrounded by *Catharanthus roseus*; pink mandevilla (right) at the patio door.

OPPOSITE: *Colocasia esculenta* 'Illustris'—also known as elephant's ear—was planted under the arbor to draw the eye toward the long view. These plants, like other tropicals on the property, are stored in a hothouse through winter. **THIS PAGE**: The walk from the north side of the property to the rear ends in a room bordered by stone walls. The inner perimeter is planted with the annual *Vinca major*.

One of a pair of metal umbrellas—patterned after the structures in Monet's garden at Giverny—acts as scaffolding for pink Meidiland roses; shades of green and pink form the palette for most of this garden. At right is a hedge of *Viburnum opulus* 'Compactum;' below is a perimeter planting of *Sedum spectabile*, more commonly known as stonecrop.

THIS PAGE: The pool house opens to the deck and creates a resort-like ambience. In addition to two large climbing hydrangeas, the building is flanked by potted Phoenix date palms. OPPOSITE: The owner uses her favorite color palette to dress the breakfast table, including small vases that showcase zinnias, variegated euonymous and ornamental grass.

e enough for croquet, the property's
culously tended lawn has been the
or many parties. It's elegant in
mplicity and a perfect platform
he grand view beyond.

THIS PAGE: Two *Nannorrhops ritchiana* and one *Dypsis decaryi*, or Triangle palm, create the look of a tropical retreat. Behind the seating area is a common boxwood hedge, pruned to resemble undulating ocean waves.
OPPOSITE: This view from the rear gate toward the back of the house shows the variations in elevation and the symmetrical plantings that enhance the home's classic architecture. A white *Rosa* 'New Dawn' twines through the arbor.

PEACEABLE KINGDOM

The landscape around the home of Nat and Lucy Day has become so well known and beloved that each year hundreds of curious visitors subscribe to the local garden conservancy's Open Days program just to have a look at the couple's green menagerie. While the garden is relatively small, it leaves a big impression in the minds of those who have seen it.

By her own admission, Lucy knew nothing about gardens when she and Nat bought a 1901 Dutch Colonial more than three decades ago. However, her strong will—which earned her a degree in archaeology and then a fine career on Wall Street—led her to plunge into what was for her uncharted territory: the world of growing things. By the time the couple had doubled the size of their property to two-thirds of an acre with the acquisition of the lot next door, Lucy was ready to make a statement with the landscape.

Fascinated with topiary, particularly those masses of yew and boxwood that have been coaxed and clipped into whimsical shapes, Lucy's first commission went to Matt Larkin. The proprietor of Black Barn Farm in western Massachusetts and a rare American practitioner of the topiary arts, Larkin crafted the Days' first topiary, a giant urn made with yew, boxwood, curly chives and creeping Jenny. It led to even wilder things.

William and Henry are a pair of ornamental lions named after the two English princes and each has a commanding presence. They are the creations of Steve Manning, a British topiarist. Manning and his wife, Jackie—a horticulturalist— spent three weeks with the Days. It took them that long to craft the lions, along with a pair of crocodiles and a trio of frogs. The Days asked the Mannings to be their houseguests while they worked on-site because it would be difficult and expensive to ship these large and complex figures overseas.

As their garden evolved, the Days became even more enamored of topiary. They asked Larkin to create several more pieces suited to their love of whimsy. Jumbo the Elephant, with his water-spraying trunk and gilt ears, was just one of the fanciful figures that enlarged the collection. Lucy herself took a turn as a topiarist; she used a nursery-bought form of buck and doe, and her own clippers, to add The Llama and His Mamma to the couple's expanding green zoo.

As much as the Days love the topiaries, creativity in this garden didn't end at botanical zoology, though it's an irresistible lure for guests. Lucy approached landscape design with a passion, searching out unique trees and plants that satisfied her inquisitive nature. While she and Nat enjoyed scouting nurseries near and far for exciting specimens, even the local market didn't escape her sharp eye. She was in a nearby grocery store when she spotted varieties of pineapple lily, a distinctively shaped South African plant normally hardy to zone 7, not her zone 6B property. Nevertheless, she loved the flowers and their foliage, so she snapped up every single pot in the supermarket. Fortunately, the plants responded in her garden, successfully overwintering in the ground.

Side by side with her exotics are plants, shrubs and trees of a more traditional nature. The huge flowers of a Southern magnolia have an intoxicating scent. The castor bean plant with mammoth leaves is grown from seed each year as the perfect companion for Jumbo in what Lucy calls her Jolly Green Giant garden. And a simple blooming rose creates ground cover, holding its place with sturdy beauty. The Day garden is documented in the Smithsonian Institute's Archive of American Gardens, so it's special indeed. And while its dimensions are on the intimate side, the Days continue to find space for new details in their whimsical Eden.

When the owners enlarged their property by purchasing an adjacent lot, the landscape architect came up with the idea of a sculpted hillside and gracefully curving walls. 'Flower Carpet' roses in a variety of colors fill one of its concave curves.

William and Henry flank one of the best seats in the garden. Above the bench and twining in the arbor are four varieties of *Clematis*: 'John Huxtable,' a white spring bloomer; 'Nelly Moser,' a pink variety that blooms in late spring and again in mid-August; 'Ramona,' the lavender variety seen here; and *Clematis paniculata*, another fall bloomer with white flowers.

ABOVE: From the belvedere, you can see the dog and pheasant topiaries in the foreground and the magnificent Japanese cedar (*Cryptomeria japonica*) at the end of the stone walk. **BELOW:** The oversized leaves of the castor bean plant (left); a view of azalea and *Chamaecyparis pisifera* 'Gold Mop' above the lion's head. **OPPOSITE:** Topiary crocodiles lounge next to a small pool surrounded by *Sedum rupestre* 'Angelina.'

ABOVE: Matt Larkin designed the table and chairs perched on the belvedere; the ground cover surrounding the topiaries is willow leaf cotoneaster. LEFT: *Rosa* 'Flower Carpet' Pink Supreme is a hybrid that's hardy and disease-resistant; it's also a long bloomer, flowering from June to September.

ABOVE: Jumbo the Elephant has 24-carat gold-leaf ears, and sprays water into his pond. **LEFT:** Not to be outdone, the crocodiles sport 24-carat gold-leaf teeth. The small evergreen to the left is a pond cypress, *Taxodium ascendans*. **OPPOSITE:** The owners fill containers around the property with annuals, including *Lantana camara* 'Pink Caprice,' and green and white-leafed *Dracaena reflexa* 'Varieta,' also known as Song of India.

ABOVE: A row of *Viburnum carlcephalum*, a deciduous shrub that's commonly known as fragrant snowball, is bordered by *Buxus* 'Green Mound,' and *Hosta* 'Floradora.'
BELOW: *Sempervivum tectorum* grow in the rocks around Jumbo's pond. **RIGHT:** Placed near a *Cotinus coggygria*—or smoke bush— is a seamless steel and concrete pot; when filled with soil, it is virtually unbreakable.

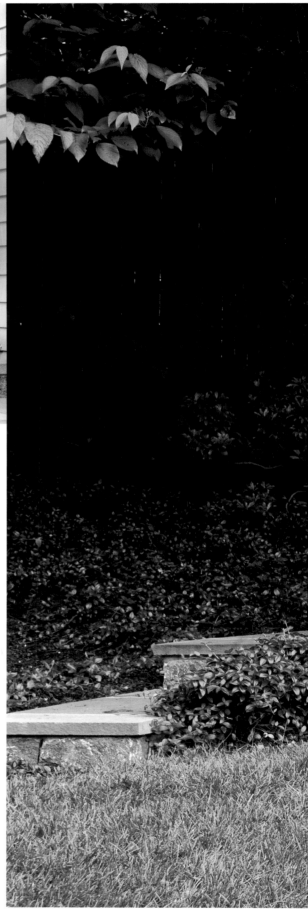

THE CONSTANT GARDENERS

rlene Scanlan was living in her home for a few years with just a small garden out back when she set her sights on the second-growth woods that took up most of her two-acre property. Envisioning a pool surrounded by a patio, a few good specimen trees and flower beds, she set to work clearing woods and thicket on a downward slope. It was an arduous process, but the rewards were worth the effort, as she was able to carve out a clear view of the sun setting over the remaining trees at the far end of her yard. It took several tries to find plants that would complement and thrive in the new landscape she had created. Arlene's initial attempt to plant a hedge around the pool was unsuccessful, but boxwoods did the trick. Fortunately, other early choices— including Japanese maples—created balance and helped define the perimeters of the garden.

Ten years after she enlarged the garden, Arlene added a pool house for her husband, David Squires, to use as a studio for his music and sculpture. It provided the couple with another setting in need of gardening. They added window boxes brimming with flowers, a wisteria-covered arbor on the path to the studio door, and perennial beds. The couple also turned one of their imaginings into reality: a delightful allée behind the studio composed of some vigorous crepe myrtles.

Since the property's sloping topography lends itself to various types of terracing, another project involved the creation of three garden rooms on the south side. Here, plantings of 'Green Giant' arborvitae along the perimeters create formal enclosures for privacy. The vertical growing habit keeps the row of trees healthy as they don't crowd each other out with horizontal branching. Within each room, focal points are created with colorful blooms—iris, roses and lilies

among them—that appear throughout the growing season. Arlene and David love the intense though brief appearance of the lilacs with their heady fragrance. She loves the round heads of the allium, which maintain their sculptural shapes even after the blooms have faded.

Although they paid careful attention to creating beds that bloom from early spring through fall, Arlene and David have never scrimped on annuals. They regularly fill the containers around the pool and the other pots that mark approaches to special areas. They put together their own containers each year, scouting their favorite greenhouse suppliers for new varieties and dependable favorites.

The couple devotes a lot of time to their garden, but early on they knew they'd need help to tend and tame the bounty of growing things. Judy Gardner had managed the gardens on the property where David had lived before he and Arlene were married, and the three had become friends. With an almost preternatural sensitivity to where a plant might best like to stay and grow, Judy has helped shape and maintain the many elements that give this garden its multilayered richness. She recently completed the installation of a white perennial garden near the pool, which the couple enjoys in the moonlight after long days at work.

Arlene and David are out back every weekend, watering, weeding, moving things and enjoying the lush environment. The couple works from 8 a.m. to 8 p.m. on Saturdays and Sundays in the summer. They are up to their eyeballs in dirt and say they love it. The trees, shrubs and perennial beds they've added have given the plot complexity and color, yet they're always thinking of new ways to expand their garden. Like most avid gardeners, this couple has never been intimidated by the thought of breaking new ground.

Plantings along the back patio that are suited for this shady site include all-green *Hosta* 'Elegans,' the green and white *Hosta* 'Fortunei Albomarginata,' and behind them, from left to right, a lavender grouping of *Nepeta racemosa*, *Iris siberica* and *Allium* 'Globemaster.' Beyond the fence is a rhododendron original to the property.

OPPOSITE: *Hydrangea anomala ssp. petiolaris* cascades over the wall that marks one boundary of three formal garden rooms. Below it is a stone spillway that carries overflow from heavy rains to the back of the sloping property. **THIS PAGE:** Rieger begonia—an indoor winter bloomer—catches a little sun outdoors; a close-up of *Allium* 'Globemaster'; and *Lupinus* 'Noble Maiden.'

Along the stairs to the back of the house from the driveway are older plantings; ferns thrive in this spot, including the large *Matteuccia struthiopteris*, or ostrich plume fern, against the fence at the left. Double hot-pink impatiens and geraniums in rosy hues fill the containers.

With their great color variety and big blossoms, dahlias such as this pink 'Fascination' really punctuate the garden.

THIS PAGE: The garden has an incredibly colorful plant life. In addition to container blooms, which the owners change each year, are standouts like the lilac standard at right. **OPPOSITE:** The owners have a nice peony collection that includes *Paeonia lactiflora* 'Gay Paree' (top); in the center of one bed (bottom) *Buxus suffruticosa*, a slow-growing dwarf variety, encircles a moss-attracting stone ball.

145

The owners asked their landscape designer to bring structure and formality to the garden rooms. *Alchemilla mollis*, *Astilbe chinensis* 'Finale' and impatiens surround the urn in the center bed; the double-tiered container is filled with a combination of plants, including *Lysimachia nummularia* 'Aurea,' and *Petunia* 'Pink Wave.' The spiky topper is *Dracaena marginata* 'Tricolor.'

OPPOSITE PAGE: A diverse arrangement of white-flowering and white- or silver-leafed species makes these garden beds glow under a waxing moon or patio lights; among the varieties blooming in the front bed are *Campanula carpatica* 'White Chips,' and *Geranium* 'St. Ola.' **THIS PAGE:** Next to the pool house/studio is an enormous cascading *Physocarpus opulifolius* 'Diablo,' a long-established purple-leafed shrub also known as Eastern ninebark.

From this perspective, levels and layers of plant growth are apparent. A perimeter planting of *Thuja* 'Green Giant' encloses the formal garden rooms; below the stone wall are more free-flowing plantings, including the fountain-like *Miscanthus sinensis* to the left. In the foreground, to the right, is the dark-leafed *Sambucus nigra* 'Black Lace.'

The westernmost formal garden room has tailored elegance, with its descending semicircular path outlined in granite block, its allée of young hornbeams and a sunrise-facing seat roofed in wisteria. A diamond-shaped boxwood border surrounds a container planted with *Tibouchina urvilleana* and *Lobelia erinus compacta* in hues of white and blue.

ROOTED IN HISTORY

Few features imbue a garden with a sense of history better than slow-growing trees that have achieved significant size and spread. Such is the case with an allée of a dozen massive pin oaks that lead to a stately home built in 1902 above a protected harbor on Long Island Sound. Here, Susan Bevan and her husband, Tony Daddino, have created a garden that honors both the scale and traditional beauty of their house and property. Many of the landscape's dramatic features—a century-old weeping cut-leaf Japanese maple, an enormous star magnolia—came with the lot when the couple bought it in 2001. The house was designed by architect Charles Alonzo Rich, and is known by its original name, Easterly. Yet when Susan and Tony took ownership, their home was in need of a garden equal to the other highlights on the two acres. Susan, a Pacific Northwest native who has loved plants since childhood, brought her own experience to the project.

Working with landscape designer Bruce Zellers, she recast the layout of the lawn that faces the Sound. One of the first things she did was remove the kidney-shaped pool, replacing it with a granite-bordered rectangular one; behind it is a vine-covered pergola that overhangs an enclosed kitchen and changing rooms. The new structures align with the scale of the home's rear elevation and create a self-contained entertaining space. Because of the property's slope, these additions aren't visible from the veranda above. Thus, the veranda retains its idyllic views of the shore. That sloping lawn also has new planting beds with generous swaths of the colorful and traditional varieties Susan loves. At the height of summer, her immense collection of daylilies creates a riot of color. She treasures them as she did the lilies that grew wild by the roadsides of her childhood home in the state of Washington.

In a large parterre that was installed to the south of the house, enclosures are filled with plants that bloom in succession through the growing season. There are masses of tulips, along with allium, multiple varieties of fern and even the same flaming scarlet *Crocosmia* 'Lucifer' that grew in Susan's mother's garden. A fountain centers this lush meditation in color and texture. Visitors to the serene spot love the space.

As they do for many properties along the southern New England coast, hydrangeas hold a particular pride of place in this garden and thrive in the salt air. Among the varieties planted are bright 'Nikko Blue' and dark purple 'Alpengluhen,' which tumble over stone walls and line paths down to the dock, where the family's boat and kayaks are kept in the warm months. Because Susan paddles out into the Sound nearly every morning in summer, her rose and clematis-covered outdoor shower was a must-have amenity.

The commanding hilltop profile of Easterly is the property's focal point. The house's elevation is vintage in nature, which is why other landscaping elements were designed with old-fashioned pleasures in mind. Antique benches in flower-filled corners entice strollers to sit and spend a few moments in quiet thought. From a giant red oak that shades the lawn, a wooden swing on a long rope promises a sweet ride and panoramic views. Tucked into a cluster of shrubs is a pair of Adirondack chairs for those in search of a place for a private conversation, and a woven hammock—straight from Tony's wish list—swings between tree trunks for lazy afternoons.

A treasure straight out of Wharton's Gilded Age, Easterly and the gardens that surround it emanate an atmosphere of elegant serenity, thanks to Susan and Tony's thoughtful stewardship and to their commitment to ensuring that this tranquil space endures for yet another century.

To protect the largest and most
susceptible branches of a century-
old weeping Japanese cut-leaf maple
from heavy snow loads, the owners
designed supports from iron bars,
curved to emulate the tree's branches.

LEFT: Easterly is approached beneath a dramatic allée of pin oak trees, on a driveway of crushed Berkshire gravel edged with Belgian block. **BELOW:** Just beyond Easterly's porte cochere is a giant Kousa dogwood. Beyond it, one of three Blue Atlas cedars was planted in honor of Susan's father and grandfather, both of whom graduated from the University of Washington with degrees in forestry.

On the south side of the house are masses of perennials and a few carefully placed ornaments, including an antique armillary.

OPPOSITE: This *Hemerocallis* hybrid is just one of dozens of varieties in the daylily garden. **THIS PAGE:** From this angle, the structural components at the south side of the house are apparent. Parterre borders are punctuated with boxwoods in pyramid shapes and spiral topiary. The low border was created with *Buxus* 'Green Velvet'; the shaped elements are 'Green Mountain.'

161

ABOVE: A *Hemerocallis* hybrid and hydrangea in flower. **BELOW:** The sunken garden parterre, which provides a private space for meditation, is centered by a fountain and antique bench shaded by a magnificent *Magnolia x soulangeana*. Red *Crocosmia* 'Lucifer' is at left.

ABOVE: The columned veranda is sheltered by an ancient and massive wisteria that blooms twice a season and enhances an all-weather location from which to enjoy the views. BELOW: This garden is colorfully diverse with *Echinacea purpurea* 'Red Knee High'; Japanese painted fern; and *Geranium* 'Johnson's Blue.'

From the lawn above the pool area, the owners can watch boats moving through the harbor. The wrought iron gates and fencing were custom-made with bronze acorn finials as a tribute to the pin oak allée.

OPPOSITE: New annuals are added to the garden each year, including this unusual pink-green petunia, 'Pretty Much Picasso.' **THIS PAGE:** The pool house is flanked by *Miscanthus sinensis* 'Gracillimus,' a distinctive and elegant grass.

The boxwood knot garden in the parking court is filled in summer with pink and orange New Guinea impatiens that are interspersed with silvery *Artemesia stelleriana*; these are preceded in spring by pansies and followed by purple and white kale in cold weather.

COMING UP ROSES

Linda Andros fondly recalls her grandmother's reputation for growing the biggest roses in Oklahoma—not an insignificant accomplishment in that hot, dry part of the country. While Linda admits the flowers may not have been quite as large as she remembers them from her childhood, the beauty and fragrance of the showy, old-fashioned French cabbage roses left a lasting impression on her.

As an adult, the singer and media executive remained fascinated by plants. When she and her husband, Bill Avery, lived in Manhattan, she'd dabble in gardening at their weekend place outside the city. Then, the couple's work took them to England, where Linda intensified her relationship with gardens; she inherited the one that came with her new home in that country. The Italian gardener who tended it, Frank Alessi, became Linda's first tutor, giving her advice about growing her favorites—roses, of course—and other plants. Friends Linda made in her new home joined Frank in this encouragement, especially three women who were dedicated gardeners themselves. They gave her pointers and visited some of England's most celebrated public gardens together.

When they moved back to the States a few years later, Linda and Bill found a vintage 1927 home and grounds. The previous owners had covered the half-timbered oak sheathing of the beautiful old Tudor house in white paint, and they used an ancient barn on the property as a pool house. Since the sellers had summered elsewhere, the garden bloomed only in spring, with a few rhododendrons and azaleas. Linda set to work immediately restoring the house to its original English style, and she got busy in the garden.

One of her English friends sent her the first rose bushes—David Austin varieties—for her new home. Remembering the conservatories in England, she designed a pool house that resembled those structures to replace the old barn. Gradually, the landscape came together. Working area by area, Linda sketched her ideas, marked her plots with string and planted. She created a seating area at the back of the house, alive with flowering plants, bushes and the birds and butterflies they attracted. She developed paths through the property, including one that led to a parterre just outside the back entrance to the house. Here, she installed a birdbath that now doubles as a pedestal on which Linda rotates the couple's collection of small sculptures they gathered while traveling.

Her roses are everywhere: climbers, shrubs and a long parade of some of her favorites in front of the pool house. Clematis, hydrangea and hellebores have captured her attention, too. As for the two pots of elegant crape myrtle, Linda says they're a challenge to grow in the Northeast, but she's not averse to an experiment. That curious nature is evident elsewhere on her property, in a place that was once used as a refuse heap; it's been transformed into a Japanese-style meditation garden where Linda goes to reflect after a busy day.

By her own admission Linda is an obsessive gardener, yet her love for nature also leads her to provide for some local habitat. Two acres of the property are left to grow untamed for the area's wildlife and the couple's bee colonies, which Bill has tended for the past several years. She eagerly shares her own knowledge, and is dedicated to practices and materials that respect and sustain the environment. Her commitment has made her a force for education and preservation in her town. It's not surprising that she offers her garden as a location for charitable fundraising events. Visitors who walk the paths she's created are awakened to her inspired vision of the natural world, which is like a rose without a thorn.

Flanking the archway leading to the back of the house are a pair of *Hydrangea quercifolia* 'Snow Queen.' The beautiful red blossoms of the *Rosa grandiflora* 'Wild Blue Yonder' in the lower right garden bed hint at what is to come. The gates are original to the 1927 house.

The owners bought
the deep red Jackson &
Perkins roses that form the
background hedge about
15 years ago; they came
in 3-inch pots. Other rose
types include the pale pink
double 'Knock Out' and
the deeper pink 'Poulbella'.
Covering the arbor are
'Zephirine Drouhin' climbing
roses, a variety from
the 19th century.

OPPOSITE: Two varieties of clematis, 'Jackmanii' and 'Niobe,' climb a trellis, and impatiens and nemesia fill a nearby pot. **THIS PAGE:** 'Dark Lady' is a David Austin rose; a close-up of a trumpet honeysuckle, *Lonicera sempervirens*; and an antique urn filled with hydrangea and vinca vine.

An African Shona sculpture sits on a granite birdbath surrounded by a parterre. The walkway is paved with marble chips and bordered by dwarf boxwood hedges. Deep pink roses are David Austin 'Dark Lady;' the yellow rose is 'Michelangelo'. *Platycodon grandiflorus* 'Astra Blue,' also known as balloon flower, adds more color to the beds.

The owners acquired *Rosa* 'Poulbella' after it was introduced in 2001; it's part of the Cuyahoga National Parks Collection, with a medium pink, double flower. They bought several bushes at the same time, but haven't found another since; the rose lives up to its reputation as cold-hardy.

Between the pool house and another building that's used for storing garden tools is a lush assemblage
of some of the owners' favorites, including 'Endless Summer' hydrangea, double pink
'Knock Out' roses and, at far left, a pale pink 'Eden Climber' rose.

Linda Andros crafted a meditation space using elements of Japanese garden design. Existing rocks are framed with a bed of pea gravel. Diminutive *Buxus sinica* var. *insularis* 'Winter Gem' surrounds the Buddha sculpture. Behind the statue are *Acer palmatum* 'Bloodgood.'

When designing the pool house, the owners modeled it after conservatory buildings in England. The roses planted along its façade include pink 'Knock Out,' the white hybrid tea variety 'Bolero,' and 'Memorial Day,' also a hybrid tea.

UNFOLDING LANDSCAPE

Twenty years ago, the owners of a historic home on an acre in the Northeast sold it to another couple—a well-traveled pair who appreciated both the house and its setting. The new owners had ideas for the property, and as luck would have it, they quickly connected with landscape designer Cindy Shumate of Cynscape Design. She had worked with the previous owners and agreed to do improvements for her new clients, relishing the opportunity to see the garden grow.

Cindy's work on this property began within the original acre, with a formal element to match the home's 19th-century vintage. She relocated a formal boxwood parterre that had been designed in the manner of Gertrude Jekyll, a pioneering landscape architect of the early 1900s. To freshen the parterre, she centered each of its enclosures with a dwarf lilac and filled the spaces with purple flowering catmint. This elegant tableau, she believed, would be subdued in color but rich in form and texture. By moving the parterre, Cindy was able to make room for other new features, including a meditation garden of zen-like simplicity, its raked surface punctuated by conical and spherical boxwoods.

The new homeowners are collectors of fine and singular things, and this applies as much to the plants they select as it does to the furnishings in their home. When the opportunity arose for the couple to acquire first one, and then two more adjacent lots, they saw the potential to create a landscape—now five acres—with multiple vistas of depth and variety.

The first acquisition of a neighboring property provided space to develop not only a tennis court, but also a path lined with exquisite conifers juxtaposed with great drifts of long-stemmed grasses. The scale of the property enabled the owners to indulge in conifer specimens that would dwarf more compact terrain, including a parade of tall evergreens— many grown to large proportions over more than a decade. A stand of weeping atlas cedars looks as if it came straight out of the movie *Fantasia*. Cindy installed a neat ribbon of pristinely groomed gravel path that curves so visitors can catch views of the neatly trimmed spherical boxwood or the clutch of arborvitae. Adjacent to the house, she planted an orchard of fruit trees, with specimens of apple, pear and others in straight lines. She used the foundation of the dwelling that once stood on the acquired property as the perimeter for the orchard's terraced dimensions. This gives the space a modern, geometric quality—it's tailored, yet dynamic. It has become a beautiful place to stroll.

With the second parcel her clients acquired, Cindy was able to find a place for organically grown herbs and vegetables, and even a unique design for improving the yield of tomato vines. Cages for berries—enclosures with simple but pleasing lines—were added to this productive section of the garden.

The garden continued to grow and spread when the owners acquired a third piece of land. At one end of the expanded property was a rolling lawn on a downhill slope. Because the soil was moist and the grass a brilliant emerald, it was the perfect environment for willows. Today, an enormous example centers this space. With its shallow roots, the willow is destined to live a short life. That's why Cindy planted a cluster of young replacements nearby.

The owners intend to add more annual beds and more dramatic displays. As the garden expands, so does the long-term vision of this couple. They continue to plan for new plants, trees and views, far into the future, and past their own stewardship. Such is the enthusiasm and creativity of these committed gardeners, who rarely rest on their laurels.

The meditation garden was artfully composed with gravel, carefully placed stones and eight boxwoods, including the corner specimens that are pruned to a point. In the distance, a red gate under an arbor covered in the climbing *Rosa* 'New Dawn' leads to an orchard.

OPPOSITE: *Passiflora* 'White Queen.' **THIS PAGE:** Evergreens are just a few of the many beautiful conifers the owners have installed over the years. A weeping Alaskan cedar, or *Chamaecyparis nootkatensis* 'Pendula,' and two *Picea pungens*, also known as Colorado blue spruce, surround a stone sculpture.

One stunning feature of the meditation garden is a set of marble steps that lead down from a parterre designed in the style of 19th-century landscape architect Gertrude Jekyll. Uphill and in the distance at right is a field of *Hakonechloa macra* 'Aureola,' or Japanese forest grass.

THIS PAGE: The *Cosmos sulphureus* (left) and *Rudbeckia hirta* 'Prairie Sun' (right) were planted in a large bed of annuals. *Allium* 'Millenium' (center) can be found in the perennial garden near the pool. **OPPOSITE:** Parterre beds are centered by dwarf Korean lilac standards and surrounded by *Nepeta grandiflora*. Raising their round heads in each bed are *Allium* 'Globemaster.'

The owners gathered a dozen *Hemerocallis* hybrids from various locations and placed them together in a row of beds next to the croquet lawn. Behind this stand of daylilies are two dramatic *Canna* 'Moonshine' in containers underplanted with *Ophiopogon planiscapus* 'Nigrescens.' The tree is *Acer platanoides,* a Norway maple.

The abundant flowers of bee balm—*Monarda didyma*—provide nectar for honeybees, hummingbirds and butterflies. Both the red and pink varieties of this plant thrive in perennial gardens in the Northeast, where it is a native. In the right location, this species blooms reliably from midsummer through fall.

A backdrop of *Miscanthus sinensis gracillimus*, or fountain grass, along with a pair of dwarf Alberta
spruce grow along one side of the pool. At the edge of this planting bed are clusters of *Euphorbia* 'Diamond Frost.'
This annual also is used in the planter with *Brugmansia versicolor* and trailing *Plectranthus coleoides* 'Variegata.'

In this perennial bed are pink *Monarda*, clusters of *Echinops ritro*, *Cornus alba* 'Elegantissima,' *Phlox paniculata* 'David,' and *Eupatorium rugosum* 'Chocolate.' *Rosa* 'Knock Out Red' centers the diverse grouping of smaller plants, including the lacy *Achillea ptarmica* in the foreground, with its button-like white flowers.

The orchard of apple, pear and other fruit trees is laid out in a geometric pattern on a terraced foundation that was once the perimeter of a house that stood here. The sculpted quality of this arrangement makes it a lovely setting for outdoor entertaining.

This grouping of *Picea glauca* 'Conica', or dwarf Alberta spruce, is affectionately known as "the family," and watched over by a dramatic grove of larger *Pinus strobus*, or Eastern white pine. The spruce needles have a densely packed growth habit that gives them a soft appearance.

Along the path to the tennis courts is a spectacular assortment of evergreens. Highlights include the row of three sculpted *Ilex crenata* 'Helleri' and, to their right, the *Juniperus* 'Pfitzer,' pruned to show off its beautiful structure.

GARDEN REFERENCE GUIDE

drawings by **JAMES GERRITY**

One of the joys of a beautiful garden is the opportunity it presents to be thoroughly explored. This section is designed in that spirit. Because it offers detailed information on each of the properties photographed for this book, it's an excellent cross-reference to the main chapters. It's not intended to be used as a garden planner, but it does serve as a valuable tool for those who want to dig deeper into the landscapes. For visuals, there are hand-drawn sketches by James Gerrity. He presents a bird's-eye view of each property so readers can gain a broader understanding of all the elements, and how they relate to one another. Photographs by Stacy Bass complement the sketches. Her images show how some of the features highlighted in the drawings looked through her lens when she was working in the gardens; arrows indicate where she was standing to compose the shots. Note the compass rose on each page; it can be used to find East, and determine where the light was coming from when Stacy captured each scene at daybreak. This section also includes words by Judy Ostrow, who offers insight on how the gardens took shape, and details that make them unique.

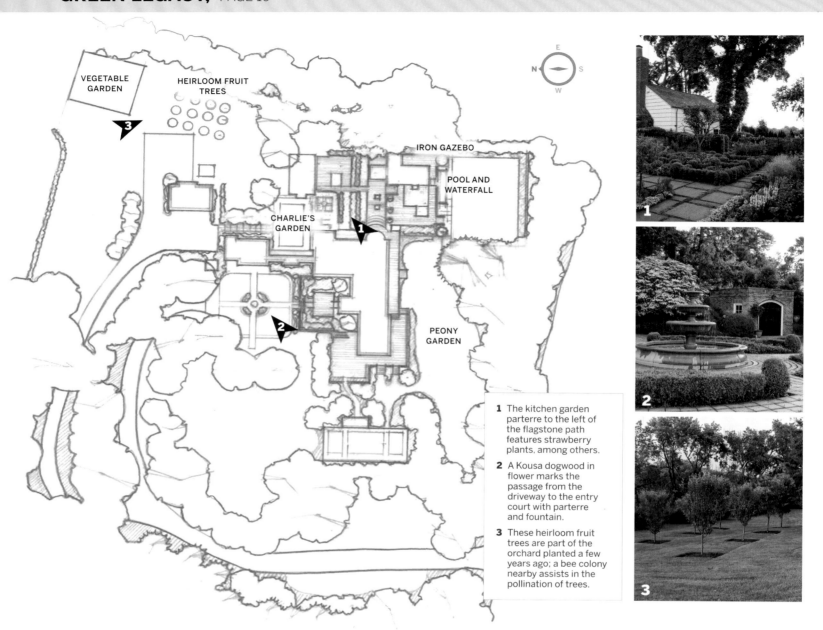

VEGETABLE GARDEN

HEIRLOOM FRUIT TREES

3

IRON GAZEBO

POOL AND WATERFALL

CHARLIE'S GARDEN

1

2

PEONY GARDEN

1 The kitchen garden parterre to the left of the flagstone path features strawberry plants, among others.

2 A Kousa dogwood in flower marks the passage from the driveway to the entry court with parterre and fountain.

3 These heirloom fruit trees are part of the orchard planted a few years ago; a bee colony nearby assists in the pollination of trees.

Overwintering Tips The Dunns have many beautiful plants that need to be kept warm in the cold months. They use two garage bays for maintaining huge Robellini palms, hibiscus, gardenia, brugmansia, agapanthus, mandevilla and other tropicals; the couple's beloved plumbagos have wintered there, too. The garage bays have ceiling grow lights and a row of windows in the top panel of the doors, as well as one electric radiator-style heater. Geraniums and succulents are transported to the kitchen solarium. Into the greenhouse—heated with a natural gas burner—go more succulents, geraniums, a gardenia, mandevilla and ivy; space also is reserved for seedlings from the vegetable garden. The efforts to maintain these warm-weather-loving plants have been successful. Many plants are now more than 10 years old. The oldest overwintered specimen is a tropical *Philodendron bipinnatifidum* 'Xanadu,' which is more than 30 years old.

Helpful Hydrangeas Jane Dunn says when you're putting a garden together and don't have a grand plan, go with hydrangeas until you do. With beautiful foliage and an abundant blooming habit, these plants are versatile and showy. Each type has certain landscape-enhancing attributes. The white *Hydrangea arborescens* 'Annabelle' has huge heads and can be cut to the ground after frost sets in, blooming the next season no matter how low the winter temperature goes. Two of the mophead varieties— *Hydrangea macrophylla* 'Nikko Blue' and 'Endless Summer'—have large blue heads that can be turned to pink by increasing the alkalinity of the soil. 'Endless Summer' blooms in early summer and again later in the season, though Jane finds a hot summer can wilt or deter the second flowering. Macrophylla varieties are vulnerable in harsh winters and may bloom sparsely or not at all the next season. Jane likes the large-blooming *Hydrangea quercifolia* (or oak leaf hydrangea)

because it has a more conical bloom and looks great at the back of a perennial bed.

Espalier Trees Almost any woody plant can be trained to grow along a flat plane, although fruit trees seem to adapt better to this type of pruning than other plants. Jane has pear trees beside a brick wall in Charlie's garden (named for a beloved dog); since masonry walls will retain heat, they can advance fruit ripening and lengthen a growing season for some plants. Other than fruit-tree espaliers, Jane also has a Southern magnolia espalier in her kitchen garden, which keeps its large and beautiful green leaves through the winter, then blooms in summer. On a lattice in the front courtyard there's a *Pyracantha* 'Mohave.' A member of the rose family, it flowers in spring and sets its berry-like pomes in the fall. All espalier plants require training and pruning in the spring, summer and autumn months by a skilled gardener.

1 This landscape design began with plantings beside the cottage that's now used as a pool and guest house.

2 The massive oak at the center of the photo is just one of the property's old and well-tended deciduous trees.

3 Between the back of the house and the shoreline are many rock outcroppings that have become perennial beds.

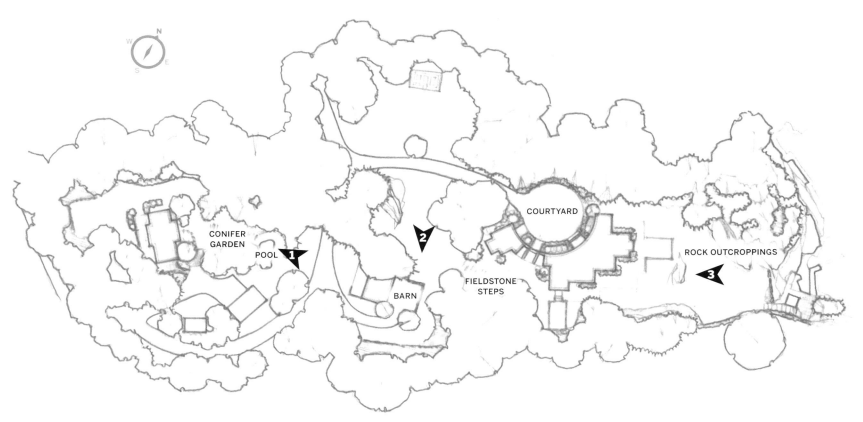

Dependable Species This garden features pretty specimen trees, including Kousa dogwood (*Cornus kousa*), also called Korean or Japanese dogwood. It's often used as a replacement for the white-flowering dogwood (*Cornus florida*), a native species in the Northeastern United States. Athracnose disease has decimated *Cornus florida* in recent years. Resistant to the fungus, Kousa dogwood blooms about a month later, and its blooms endure longer than those of the native species. In addition to its other distinctions from *Cornus florida*, Kousa has pointed bracts rather than rounded ones. Fall foliage is a showy red, with edible red berry clusters.

Rock Gardens The rock outcroppings on this property, with their natural shapes and flow, make great base material for perennial and annual beds. The terrain is reminiscent of coastal areas in Maine and California, where rock gardens are common. Landscape designer Heather O'Neill likes to leave some crannies exposed and fill others with soil. She reserves shallow spaces for annuals and likes to add some creepers to the mix, such as *Phlox stolonifera*, which has horizontal shoots that help it colonize easily. Other choices are sedum, dianthus and portulaca for splashes of color. When choosing plants, Heather takes wind into consideration, but has observed that plants seem to adapt. As with establishing any sort of bed, patience is required. It takes a few years for a rock garden to get settled.

Winter Structure The natural beauty of this waterfront location will enhance the stark grays and browns of winter, but even so, the owners planned for some added interest when flowering season is finished. To add mass and structure during cold weather months, evergreens in different shades of green and with varying needle textures were installed. Among the many evergreens chosen were *Chamaecyparis obtusa* (hinoki cypress), with its feathery-looking leaves, and *Sciadopitys verticillata*, or Japanese umbrella pine, named for the growth habit of its foliage. Both look great under snow cover. Deciduous trees also create interest in the cold months. A notable deciduous tree in this garden is the coral-bark maple (*Acer palmatum* 'Sango-kaku'), which also adds color to the landscape. When cutting back plants and bushes, the owners will leave in place some of the drying hydrangea flowers and grasses that have turned tan as they provide a visual break in the landscape and a place for birds to rest.

Soil Enrichment What's the key ingredient of the rich black soil in this garden? Owner Phoebe Cole-Smith says it's all about compost. The soil is enriched with kitchen scraps. Compost is made with only vegetable waste, plus tea leaves, eggshells and coffee grounds. Phoebe puts no meat or dairy on the pile, as these attract rodents.

Garden Hens In addition to providing eggs, the hens act as a natural pesticide for the garden, eating mosquitoes, leaf-munching larvae and other destructive insects. As an added benefit, chicken manure is one of the best possible natural fertilizers for a garden, but it must be aged. Chicken droppings are loaded with nitrogen, which can be too "hot" and cause young plants to wither. The owners set the manure aside before adding it to the garden. They age their

pile for a year, though some gardeners say that turning the manure can ready the fertilizer in less time, as quickly as four to six months.

Tapping Maple Trees Sugar maples cover three of the five acres here. Getting maple syrup from sap is a labor-intensive process. According to Mike Smith, the ratio of sap to syrup in gallons is about 40:1, although it varies by sugarbush. The maples in this garden generally provide syrup at a ratio of 42:1. A maple tree is ready for tapping when it's 12 inches in diameter; it can sustain two taps at 20 inches diameter. The best conditions for sap flow are when the daytime temperatures are 45 degrees Fahrenheit and the nighttime temps drop to 25 degrees F. Warm days and freezing nights are the ideal combination. Syrup season in southern

Connecticut (where this garden is located) usually starts on February 1 and can last until April 1.

Herbs and Heirloom Plants In this garden, old varieties of plants are cultivated when the owners gather seeds to grow the next generation. They grow flowers, vegetables and herbs with heirloom seeds, a practice being adopted worldwide. Radishes are Phoebe's personal favorite, and she has the best luck with two heirlooms: *Raphanus savitus* 'Cherry Belle' and *Raphanus sativus* 'French Breakfast'. Phoebe says that the leaves of this vegetable are delicious if they're perky and fresh, and can be added to salads or sautéed. As for herbs, Phoebe likes the easy-to-grow chervil (*Anthriscus cerefolium*), best used raw in delicate salads and vinaigrettes.

1 The owners' productive bee colonies live in hives tucked away in a corner that's not too far from the house.

2 The flowers from this garden are used for bouquets that decorate the dining table, where Phoebe's home-grown food is served.

3 Artisan Bill Howe of Connecticut crafted an enclosure for this space that is both aesthetic and functional.

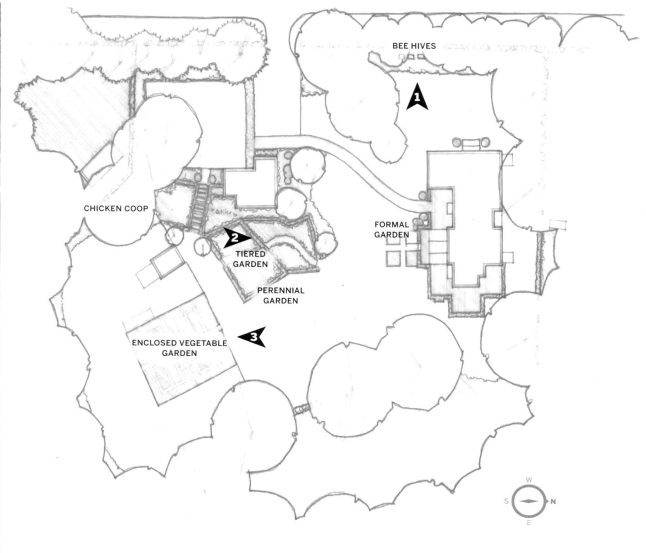

BEE HIVES

CHICKEN COOP

FORMAL GARDEN

TIERED GARDEN

PERENNIAL GARDEN

ENCLOSED VEGETABLE GARDEN

Successful Clematis There are many different forms of clematis with a wide array of habit, vigor and flower type. Some are repeat bloomers, and some bloom over a long period of time. To find a site for clematis, landscape designer Kim Proctor says follow the old adage: Feet in the shade and head in the sun. The clematis along the sunny, south-facing wall of the Macleod-Klee sunken garden have their feet in the shade as roots are kept cool with the coverage of salvia and spiraea in the bed. Clematis is generally not happy with soil that's too acidic, so lime can be used to "sweeten" it. These beautiful, flowering vines, once established, can bloom for many years.

Palette and Structure When Kim was researching the gardens of Agnes Selkirk Clark and the designer's mentor, Ellen Biddle Shipman, it was clear to her that the original garden would have been planted in the English tradition for dense perennial beds. These would have had a wide variety of plants to assure a succession of blooms throughout the growing season. This style does require a tremendous amount of maintenance, however. Kim's goal was to limit the work involved in this sunken garden. For that reason, she created a carefully edited palette of mostly blues and purples, with white and a bit of pink and yellow. Using plants with varied foliage, she was also able to achieve an array of greens that add to the beds' texture and form. Today, the garden looks sharp in all of the growing months.

Multiple Microclimates The sunken garden possesses at least four microclimates within its walls. Along its north side is a very hot, full-sun situation. To the east, under the pergola, there is part shade and then deep shade under the dogwood and hedges. Finally, in the southeastern corner of the garden is a very damp environment. Thus, the plant selection for this area could not be as symmetrical as the garden itself looks on paper. Instead, bright areas were planted with more sun-loving varieties, while the damper, darker parts of the layout were suited for different types of plant material. Gardeners and designers alike will often say that placement is much more key to a plant's success than any other factor. In order to thrive, plants need to be compatible with their surroundings.

1 Mounds of salvia and other sun-and heat-loving plants occupy the warmer and drier portions of the beds in the sunken garden.

2 A footpath beyond the formal portion of the landscape was installed to provide an extended view of the fields in the distance.

3 Rounds created with foundation plantings and artful containers create curvy counterpoints to the Craftsman-style house.

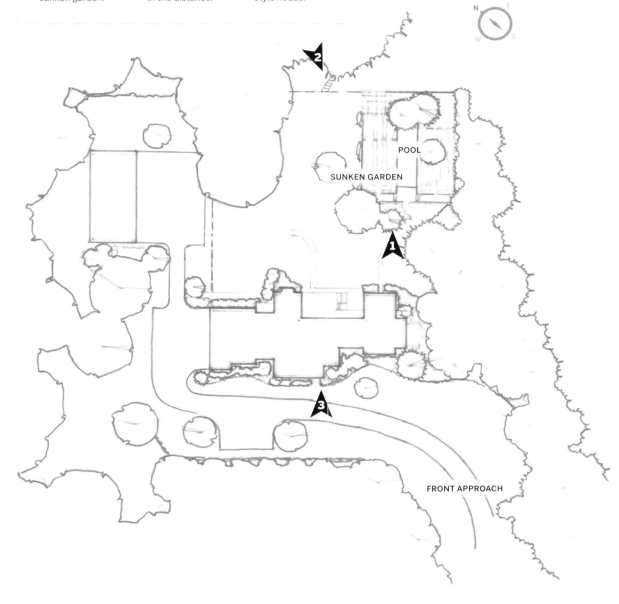

Seaworthy While some seaside home elevations are thoroughly exposed to the spray and salt, landscape architect Sean Jancski says the Bass property is upland of the water's edge, with an existing timber seawall, and not typically subject to tidal issues. So, instead of selecting seashore plants, tried-and-true hardy varieties were installed, and they've done well. These include Manhattan euonymus espalier (*Euonymus kiautschovicus* 'Manhattan'), Hameln Fountain Grass (*Pennisetum alopecuroides* 'Hameln'), and Nikko Blue Hydrangea (*Hydrangea macrophylla* 'Nikko Blue'), a mainstay of coastal New England.

Up Front Because the house massing has character and scale, Sean wanted to create drama with the landscape. While most homes in this neighborhood have traditional front foundation plantings, his strategy was to bring more of the plantings out toward the street, creating a front-yard room with three pocket gardens. This approach creates a strong boundary between the road and the house. For residents of the house, it makes for a more interesting view from the inside looking out.

Right Evergreens Evergreens have different growth habits, and the key to creating a good perimeter screen with these trees is to select the right variety, keeping balance and texture in mind. The evergreens planted in the front of the Bass house are Emerald arborvitae (*Thuja occidentalis* 'Emerald') and Common American Boxwood (*Buxus sempervirens*). Sean says the Emerald arborvitae was essential in the design because it creates a natural green wall of privacy. The tall, upright habit of the arborvitae allows for planting the trees close together, making for a solid hedge. Arborvitae also complements a structured landscape design. Boxwoods in front of arborvitae can soften the effect of the green wall; they can also be closely spaced to create a low hedge. Here, boxwoods frame the pocket gardens, emphasizing the sculptures and seating areas.

Soft Hardscape There are many weed-free spaces between pavers in various parts of this landscape. That's accomplished with the use of creeping thyme (*Thymus serpyllum*), a low-growing ground cover that obviates the need for herbicides or hand-weeding the gaps between stones. Other plants useful for this purpose are creeping phlox (*Phlox stolonifera*), dwarf periwinkle (*Vinca minor*), hens and chicks (*Sempervivum*) and creeping jenny (*Lysimachia nummularia*).

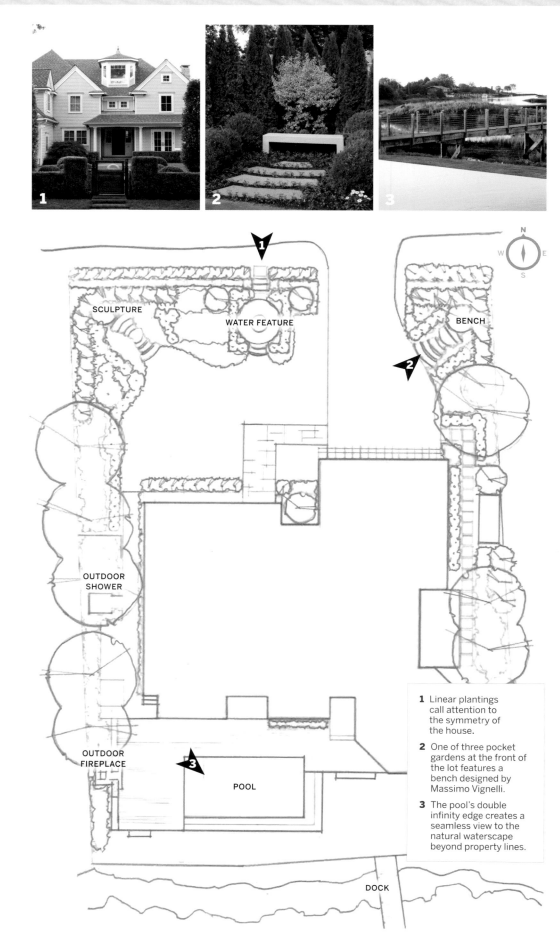

1 Linear plantings call attention to the symmetry of the house.

2 One of three pocket gardens at the front of the lot features a bench designed by Massimo Vignelli.

3 The pool's double infinity edge creates a seamless view to the natural waterscape beyond property lines.

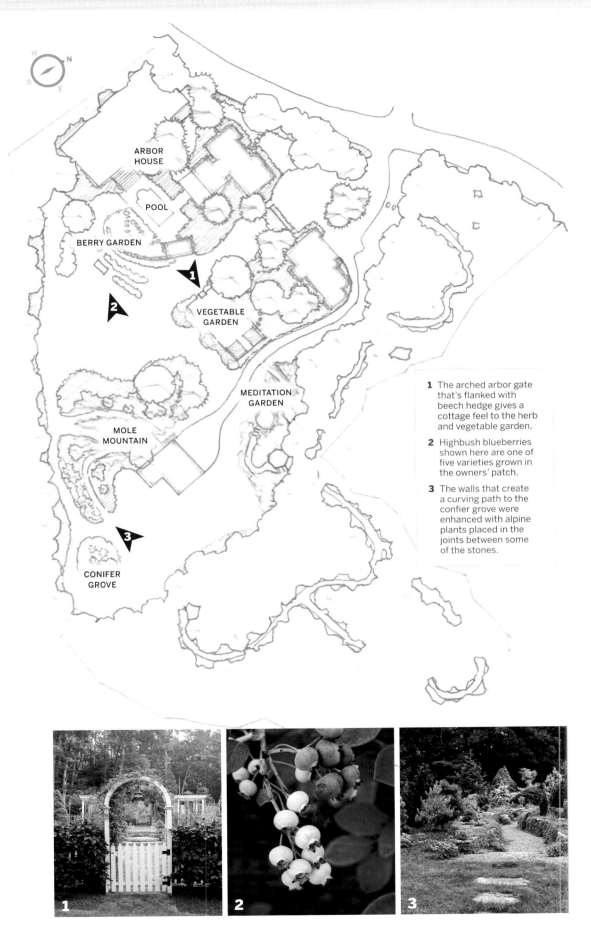

ARBOR
HOUSE

POOL

BERRY GARDEN

1

2

VEGETABLE
GARDEN

MEDITATION
GARDEN

MOLE
MOUNTAIN

3

CONIFER
GROVE

1 The arched arbor gate
that's flanked with
beech hedge gives a
cottage feel to the herb
and vegetable garden.

2 Highbush blueberries
shown here are one of
five varieties grown in
the owners' patch.

3 The walls that create
a curving path to the
conifer grove were
enhanced with alpine
plants placed in the
joints between some
of the stones.

Deer Control The area surrounding the Larneds' property includes hundreds of acres of state preservation land where deer roam freely. A combination of neighboring electric and wire fences and the Larneds' own electric deer fence protect all but the north boundary of the landscape. Though the front lawn and foundation plantings are undefended, they're enhanced with material the deer find unpalatable, such as cultivars of Japanese andromeda (*Pieris japonica*), as well as Japanese cedar (*Cryptomeria*), spirea and daffodils. Since no fence is foolproof, the Larneds also planted arborvitae, yew and hosta—all of which are excellent deer bait—at a few locations near enclosures. These serve as "canary in the coal mine" species, meaning they help the owners detect deer infiltration as the animals are lured to nibble on what they consider to be attractive plants.

Busy Bees Six of the 12 gardens in this book are home to honeybee colonies, and Michael Larned is perhaps the most senior beekeeper of all the homeowners, having begun in 1992. His harvests of berries, apples and vegetables are larger due to the on-site bee colonies. There's labor involved in keeping bees, but an appealing benefit is honey. A typical colony can produce up to 75 pounds a year. While the news is full of alarming reports of Colony Collapse Disorder (a serious problem threatening the health of honeybees and the economic stability of commercial beekeeping in the U.S.), the Larneds say none of the beekeepers in their locale have encountered this problem. More common reasons for colony die-off are starvation in cold winters and infestations of mites.

Conifer Collection Michael has collected several hundred varieties of conifer, typically defined as a bush or tree that produces cones and often has leaves that are green all year. Yet one of the most special varieties in his garden is the Japanese umbrella pine (*Sciadopitys verticillata*), which was on the property when Michael and his wife bought it. Since the Larneds took ownership of the land, the original specimen has more than doubled in size, to about 23 feet. Michael planted this species at each of the three entrances to the conifer/alpine garden. A grove located behind this garden is the only space on the property devoted purely to conifers. Michael created it to enjoy a selection of specimens that contrast in form and color. Typically they are larger trees, not classified as miniature or dwarf. The grove includes distinctive varieties of cedar, cypress, spruce, pine, arborvitae and juniper.

1

2

3

Borrowing Landscape Controlling the height, width and placement of trees, hedges and fences can be advantageous if the views beyond the lot lines provide a scenic vista. For instance, if you trim a tree just right, you can uncover a view of a neighbor's property that flatters your own without sacrificing privacy. The Faths were on the receiving end of just such a bonus prospect. When their neighbors removed some old hemlocks, they picked up views of Long Island Sound located several miles away. The part of the Fath's landscape that allows the view is always kept open to this lovely reveal.

Haute Hedge Designer Rob Wilber used a significant amount of hedge for the garden rooms and other edged features. To keep hedges—especially boxwood—looking their best, it's critical to do three things. First, carefully plan the time of pruning, since air temperature and other factors have an effect. Second, the inside or center of the plant needs airflow to discourage pests and disease. A well-pruned hedge will have small openings in it to allow for this; artful hand pruning makes this kind of clipping invisible. Finally, soil pH needs to be consistent for the full length of the hedge to prevent discoloration or variations in leaf color.

Water Features In addition to the fountain that's centered on the back terrace—where it forms a point on the long axis from the rear of the house to the back of the pool area—the owners wanted to add more flowing water to the landscape design. Their idea was to create a gentle stream of water along the low walls that border the terrace. Landscape designer Alice Cooke, who created new foundation and front elevation plantings, loved this idea of a water wall. The feature she made is a great addition to the property; the barely perceptible trickle of water over the stones in the wall is cooling and soothing on a hot summer day. The water is operated off of the irrigation system and runs through a series of small hoses that feed to the back of the wall just under the capstone. The water runs down the face of the stones and into a rill, which collects and then deposits water into a pipe hidden behind the lower corner of the terrace. The pipe drains water to an old well that's located on the edge of the property.

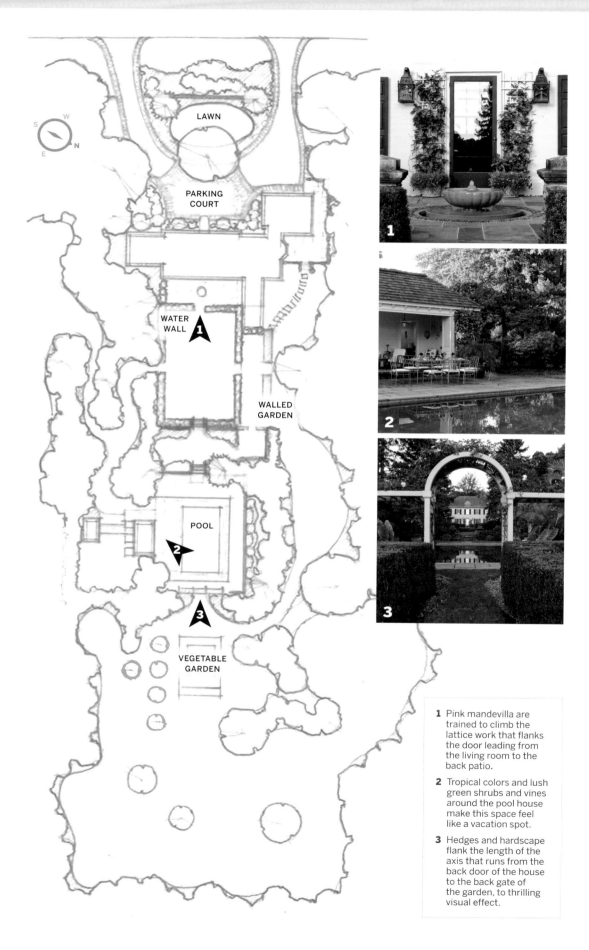

1 Pink mandevilla are trained to climb the lattice work that flanks the door leading from the living room to the back patio.

2 Tropical colors and lush green shrubs and vines around the pool house make this space feel like a vacation spot.

3 Hedges and hardscape flank the length of the axis that runs from the back door of the house to the back gate of the garden, to thrilling visual effect.

Topiary Facts Topiary—the art of trimming and training plants into three-dimensional, ornamental shapes—has been practiced for centuries but is relatively uncommon in the United States. The topiaries in this garden were constructed with metal forms to shape the underlying plants (usually boxwood or yew). The lions William and Henry were crafted with grass; golden dwarf sweet flag (*Acorus gramineus* 'Ogon') was used for manes and tails. Maintenance is not labor intensive; the grass coat of each lion is trimmed with special clippers when the lawn is mowed. Boxwood and yew grow relatively slowly and are clipped when needed, about twice a year. In winter, the lions' grass goes dormant; all of the topiaries look lovely with a coating of snow.

Viewing Place Owners Nat and Lucy Day enjoy a stroll around their garden path to admire its engaging features. Early on, the couple noticed that a particular point in the path offered a fine panorama of the landscape. They asked a craftsman to make an artful table and chairs for this spot and christened it the belvedere, or "beautiful sight." A well-placed and appropriately scaled structure where one can rest and observe a garden's beauty is always a fine idea.

Magnificent Specimens Dramatic trees punctuate a landscape, particularly rare varieties. This property has a huge southern magnolia. Also known as *Magnolia grandiflora* 'Edith Bogue,' it's the most cold-hardy cultivar the owners could find. Relatively rare in northern climes, it boasts large, deep-green leaves with a waxy coating and plate-sized (up to 12 inches in diameter) white flowers with a citrus fragrance. The magnolia has been moved three times since it was first planted more than 25 years ago, largely to accommodate renovation projects. It's currently in a sheltered spot and continues to provide interest, color and fragrance.

Ground Cover Many gardeners use an easy-care ground cover for sloping sites that are difficult to mow; pachysandra and vinca are often used to fill in such places. The owners of this garden chose the willow leaf cotoneaster (*Cotoneaster salicifolius repens*). Pest-resistant and quick-growing, it bears red berries in the fall if planted in full sun; cold winters turn green leaves to reddish-purple. The plant is drought tolerant and needs no special fertilizer.

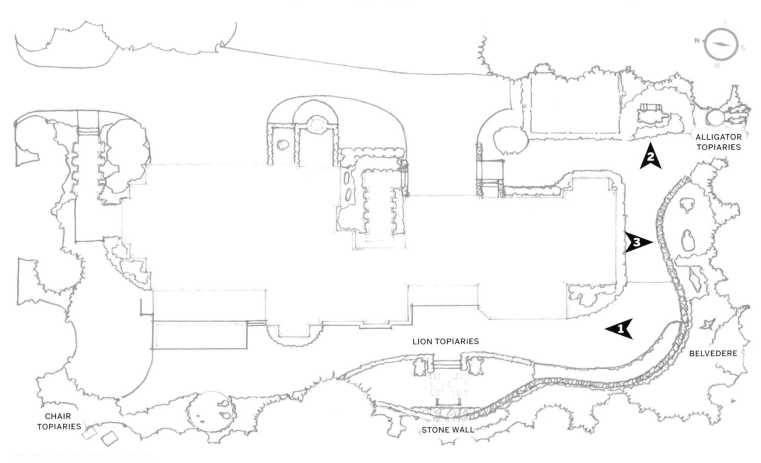

ALLIGATOR TOPIARIES

LION TOPIARIES

BELVEDERE

CHAIR TOPIARIES

STONE WALL

1 This elevated view from the garden's belvedere reveals the appealing serpentine curve of the stone walls.

2 Jumbo's trunk streams water to a nearby recirculating pond and never fails to produce a smile from those who see him.

3 All of the topiaries, including the hunting dog—a tribute to Nat Day's love of the sport—are illuminated in the evening.

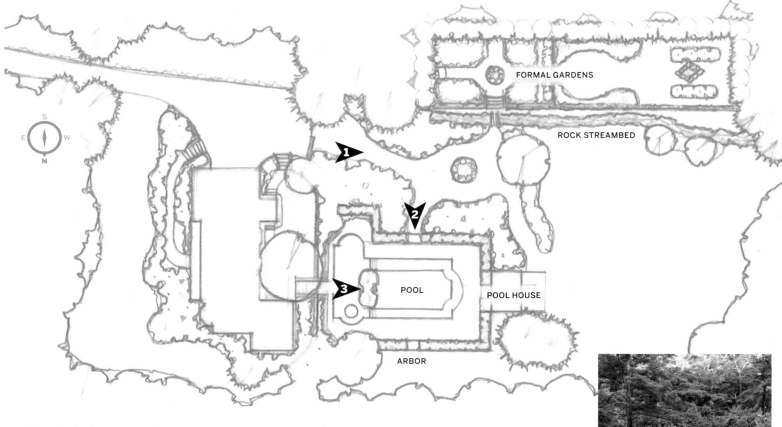

FORMAL GARDENS

ROCK STREAMBED

POOL

POOL HOUSE

ARBOR

Man-Made Streambed A fieldstone streambed was constructed to function like a gutter and divert water away from the garden. The property is at the bottom of a steeply pitched street, and the parcel itself is on a downward slope; this condition would leave water standing on the owners' acreage after a heavy rain. The couple owns the woods at the end of the slope, so the water can run safely off the maintained section of the property. When it's not carrying excess rainfall away from the lush gardens, the streambed is an attractive feature on its own.

Containers Planting annuals in pots, urns and other vessels is a great, low-maintenance method for adding color and texture to a landscape. It's also easy for lawn companies to maintain these mini-gardens while the owners are away; just add water and deadhead as needed. The owners install all their containers around Mother's Day, including the window boxes. After that, maintenance is a matter of water and fertilizer. They use a readily available, mass-market brand of fertilizer. The soil mixture is ordinary, although depending upon the plants' requirements, they add a bit of peat moss to the mix.

Moon Garden White flowers and silver foliage have the distinction of reflecting moonlight or well-placed artificial light; when illuminated, they seem to literally glow in the dark. Since the owners frequently use the area around the pool for relaxing and entertaining in the evening, the space seemed a good location for a "moon garden," composed of white-blooming plant material. It was installed by their designer and flower guru, Judy Gardner. Among her perennial plantings are early bloomers, such as bearded iris 'Immortality' (*Iris germanica*), white delphinium (*Delphinium alba*) and white foxglove (*Digitalis alba*). Mid-season bloomers are white lupine (*Lupinus* 'Noble Maiden'); and late bloomers include the Japanese anemone 'Honorine Jobert.' There are also various white roses and shrubs. The collection creates a continuously beautiful backdrop, by day and at night.

Robust Rhododendron Evergreen shrubs tend to thrive in the acidic soils and humid summer climate of southern Connecticut, which is why the enormous rhododendrons in this garden have done extremely well, even after they were transplanted during renovations. Judy notes that a great percentage of a plant's success has to do with being planted in the right place for its needs. Here, rhododendrons thrive in the right kind of soil, good shade with dappled sun, and sufficient water that keeps the shrub's large root ball moist but not too wet.

1 Long grassy walks are a feature of the landscape; a circular parterre centered with a moss-covered sphere is the focal point for the path from the driveway.

2 The owners mark destination points with vine-covered arbors. The path to the pool also has a purple martin house to attract these insect-loving birds.

3 To accentuate the pool area, the owners fill a number of containers with annuals, including the window boxes on the pool house.

About Allées A dramatic approach to a home makes a big impression. Easterly is well-known for its allée, composed of a dozen enormous pin oaks (*Quercus palustris*). This tree has a great vertical trunk and performs well in the Northeast. Most oak varieties are too wide for this application. The scarlet oak (*Quercus coccinea*) is structurally the same, but because it holds its leaves late into winter, some landscape designers find it unsuitable for an allée. In Europe, the plane tree (*Platanus*, or, in North America, sycamore, especially *Platanus occidentalis*) is commonly used to form an allée, but it suffers from rust in a Northeastern climate and defoliates early without multiple sprayings. The American elm (*Ulmus americana*) was probably the best tree for this purpose with its tall, vase-shaped branching, but Dutch Elm disease nearly eliminated this species in the 20th century. Disease-resistant elms are in development, and designers hope to use them in the future.

Saltwater Mitigation Because this is a waterfront site with an easterly exposure, landscape designer Bruce Zellers had to compensate for the inevitable wrath of Mother Nature. After Superstorm Sandy in 2012, he treated Easterly's soil with gypsum to alter the chemical composition of the salt to calcium. Had the storm dumped more rain, salt levels would have been lowered. He estimates the treatment was about 90 percent successful.

Managing Hybrids Daylilies are easily hybridized, with thousands of varieties derived from the species *Hemerocallis*. When the home's owner Susan Bevan was living in her former house, she acquired a huge assortment of multicolored daylily hybrids from a local specialist, who planted them around the property. When she moved to Easterly, she took some of each variety with her, transplanting them successfully. During house renovations, the hybrids were moved again to avoid damage—they were put close to a neighbor's bed of native (orange) daylilies, *Hemerocallis fulva*. When renovations were complete, Susan replanted the flowers to their former beds. To her shock, orange daylilies came up the next summer. Research suggests that native daylilies will aggressively overtake hybrids, crowding them out with an underground root system. To revive her multicolored display, Susan removed the orange usurpers and replaced them with daylilies she found in nurseries. These replacements now grace her beds with an amazing show every summer.

1 The herb and vegetable garden is planted with both produce and marigolds, which keep pests under control.

2 The parking court at the front entrance is centered with an octagonal parterre, or knot garden, and accentuates the classic porte cochere.

3 The sunken garden parterre has a boxwood border pruned in a pattern to resemble that of the knot garden.

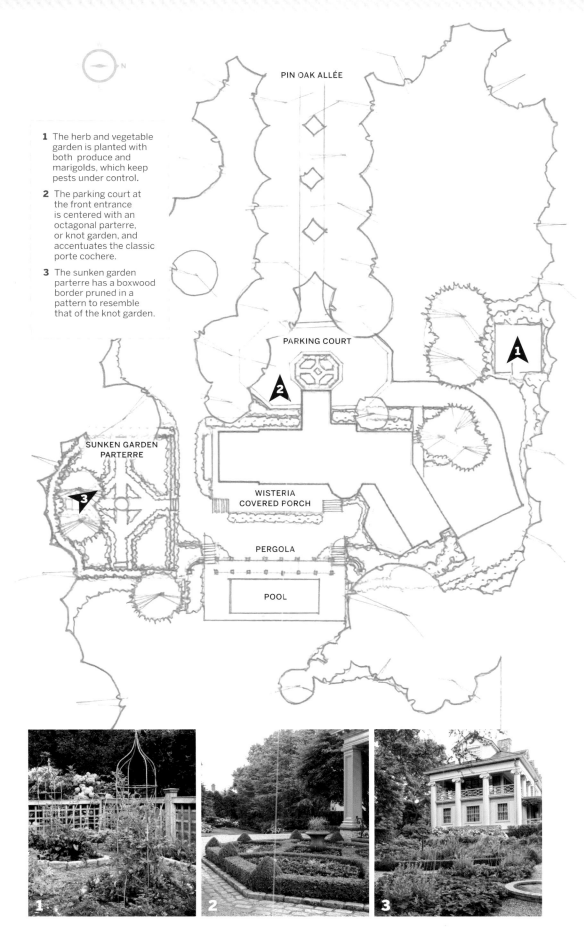

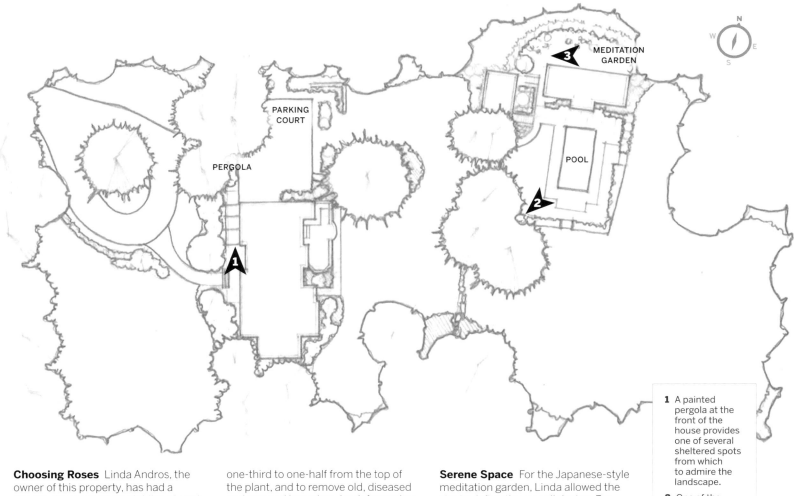

PARKING COURT

PERGOLA

MEDITATION GARDEN

POOL

1

2

3

1 A painted pergola at the front of the house provides one of several sheltered spots from which to admire the landscape.

2 One of the property's many colorful vignettes is this collection of pink blooms— mostly roses and foxglove— that's located near the pool enclosure.

3 The meditation garden, created for rest and contemplation, glows in the light of dawn.

Choosing Roses Linda Andros, the owner of this property, has had a passion for roses since childhood, and she has a great deal of experience with this beautiful flower. She suggests buying early in the season, when roses are fresh from the growers and in the best condition. The longer they sit at the nursery, the less likely they are to receive adequate care. Even when buying from a reputable garden center, always look for the obvious problems of disease and pests. In terms of varieties, 'Knock Outs' are good for those who don't have time or interest in nursing roses along. However, they still require deadheading throughout the growing season to encourage more abundant repeat blooming. *Rosa rugosa* varieties are also hardy and low-maintenance. Linda buys only repeat bloomers for her garden, but some varieties are more vigorous than others. She tries to pair roses that bloom more frequently with those that don't to maintain a steady bloom throughout the season.

Pruning Protocol Pruning shears and rosarians are constant companions. Linda follows the guidance she received early on, that the first pruning should begin when the forsythia blooms. Among several pruning theories, the one she subscribes to is to prune

one-third to one-half from the top of the plant, and to remove old, diseased and crossed branches. Look for sucker growth and remove. As the blooming period progresses, so does constant deadheading; all cuts should be at a 45-degree angle, ¼ inch above the first full leaf. Linda doesn't usually prune after the last bloom so that the rose can create its hip and naturally go into dormancy. As to growing advice, Linda says fertilize. She also heeds the counsel of her Italian gardener and friend, who taught her to just relax and prune in July and August, when the foliage turns yellow and drops off. In September, roses will regenerate.

Serene Space For the Japanese-style meditation garden, Linda allowed the site to define the overall design. For instance, she created it within existing rock formations, particularly because rocks in this type of garden are referred to as sacred stones, or *iwa kura*. (Linda uses one for her own meditation seat.) This site also is naturally shady, another traditional feature of meditation gardens. She decided not to fence in the area. Instead, she left openings between the arborvitae she planted. In this way, she can view the open fields and woods beyond, applying another Japanese principle, *shakkei*, or borrowed view.

Very Zen The classic Japanese rock garden was the template for this home's meditation garden. A feature of Zen temples in Kyoto, Japan, from the 14th through 16th centuries, the Japanese rock garden was designed to imitate nature in its essence, not actual appearance, and functioned to aid in meditation. This garden consists of carefully placed rocks, as well as pruned bushes and trees, on a bed of gravel raked to resemble rippling water. Landscape designer Cindy Shumate chose four corner plants and four interior plants with similar shapes, each placed to achieve visual balance in the rectangular space. These eight boxwoods are pruned meticulously. The gravel is maintained weekly with an aluminum rake.

Fruit Trees Orchards require consistent maintenance. On this property, there are many types of fruit-bearing trees: Asian pear trees; quince; Chinese apricot; Macintosh, Fuji, Granny Smith and Red Delicious apples; and Bing cherries. Using Cornell University Fruit Tree Pest Management guidelines, apples and pears are sprayed every 10 to 14 days in growing season, depending upon weather. Fertilizers, soil amendments and soil enhancers/nutrients are injected directly into the tree root area. Pruning of water sprouts is usually done in mid-to-late July. This allows sunlight to reach the fruit so it will ripen and achieve the desired color. More extensive pruning occurs in late winter.

Stone Pyramids Environmental sculpture by Andy Goldsworthy— acclaimed for his site-specific land art created with natural materials—was the inspiration for the four stone pyramids that are strategically located on the property to lead a visitor's eye to special views. Greg Holomakoff and Tony Caravalla of Norwalk, Connecticut, crafted the pieces.

Placement and Pruning This landscape offers several lessons in the placement and pruning of large elements to great effect. The fruit orchards, for instance, are planted on an elevated terrace in straight lines to give the property a disciplined, contemporary structure. Special attention was also given to the conifers and evergreens on this property. In the case of multiples of one species, the trees are often grouped together for a more dramatic visual effect. A tree with a great branching form, such as the prized juniper 'Pfitzer,' is more remarkable when pruned to show off its underlying structure.

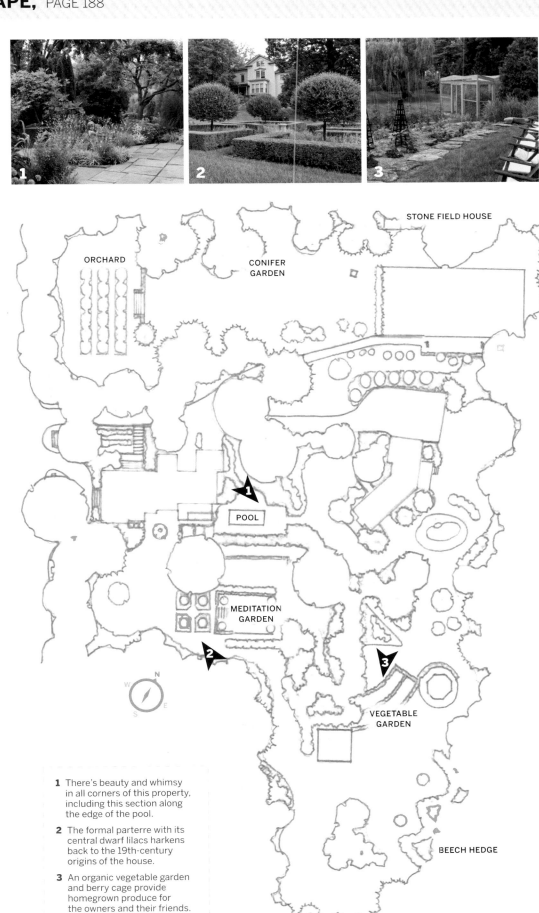

1 There's beauty and whimsy in all corners of this property, including this section along the edge of the pool.

2 The formal parterre with its central dwarf lilacs harkens back to the 19th-century origins of the house.

3 An organic vegetable garden and berry cage provide homegrown produce for the owners and their friends.

STONE FIELD HOUSE

ORCHARD

CONIFER GARDEN

POOL

MEDITATION GARDEN

VEGETABLE GARDEN

BEECH HEDGE

ACKNOWLEDGEMENTS

When I finish a book, I take great interest in reading the acknowledgements. I recognize how extraordinary it is for so many people to collaborate on a single creative project. As I write my note of thanks, I realize how uplifting it's been to have worked with a team of people who brought so many different perspectives, skills and talents to this volume.

I offer my endless gratitude to the book's executive producer and creative director, Amy Vischio, who has been a true partner in this process. You are a consummate professional and brilliant designer who settles for nothing less than the best. I am lucky to have you in my corner, and because of your talents, we benefit from the amazing way you see the world. I'm also grateful to Jonathan Moffly, president of Moffly Media. Your enthusiasm is infectious and encouraging. It's made this process a wonderful experience, from start to finish.

My thanks also to Judy Ostrow. I can't imagine a more fitting writer for this book. Your prose captures the spirit of these extraordinary landscapes; your calm, grace and thoughtfulness set the perfect tone for an exploration down each garden path. Jeanne Craig of Moffly Media has been a most excellent editor. Thank you for the energy, time and attention to each and every word. I also appreciate the tremendous efforts of the rest of the Moffly team, particularly art director Paula Winicur and production manager Kerri Fice.

I have to acknowledge the garden owners and landscape designers who have come along for this ride with me. Thank you not only for saying yes, but also for doing so with such palpable excitement and delight. The time I spent in the places you created was nothing less than inspiring. And to the talented James Gerrity, whose beautiful hand-drawn sketches create the centerpiece of our reference guide, my thanks for getting it all right. A special thank you to my dear friend and mentor Charlie Melcher, for listening to my musings and offering just the right amount of hand-holding.

Finally, I have to acknowledge my family, including my spectacular mom, Jessica Waldman, just because she deserves it. To my husband, Howard Bass, thank you for fortifying my confidence, and for your enthusiasm, advice and boundless love. Walking through this world with you is the greatest gift. And to our children, Ilysa, Benjamin, Michael and Emily: You are all bright and beautiful, kind and caring, motivated and magnetic. I'm forever grateful for you in my life. I hope I have made you proud.

DATE DUE

JUN 2 0 2015			
JUL 1 9 2015			
SEP 2 2015			
DEC 1 9 2015			
MAY 1 1 2016			
			PRINTED IN U.S.A.